MAKE OR BREAK CONVERSATIONS

How Smart Financial Professionals Land New Clients and Keep Them For Life

MARY SCHMID

INDIE BOOKS INTERNATIONAL®

Printed in the United States of America.

ISBN: 978-1-952233-25-8
Library of Congress Control Number: 2020918958

Designed by Joni McPherson, mcphersongraphics.com

INDIE BOOKS INTERNATIONAL®
2424 VISTA WAY, SUITE 316
OCEANSIDE, CA 92054
www.indiebooksintl.com

CONTENTS

Foreword v

1 Why High-Trust Conversations Are Your Competitive Advantage 1

2 Understanding The Chemistry Of Conversations 5

3 From Self-Awareness To Self-Management 21

4 Meet The Money Archetypes 35

5 The Science of Conversation: Introduction To Seven Principles 47

6 Principle #1: Share The Air 57

7 Principle #2: Respect Others' Opinions 67

8 Principle #3: Stretch Thinking 79

9 Principle #4: Discover Ideas 91

10 Principle #5: Explore Meaning 117

11 Principle #6: Speak Up 131

12 Principle #7: Success Together 159

Epilogue: Axel And The Purple Lip Gloss 171

Appendix

A. Acknowledgments 179

B. About The Author 181

C. References 183

D. Index 187

FOREWORD

As a successful entrepreneur in the wealth management and banking profession, I thought I had a pretty good idea of how to lead my teammates by using great conversations. Well, a divorce after thirty-two years and a desire to grow my all-star financial team of seven into a team of fifteen to twenty professionals that will keep All Star Financial thriving for another thirty plus years, got me thinking. *I can do better.*

A close friend of mine suggested that I talk to Mary Schmid about coaching. It was the best thing I have ever done as a professional wanting to be better. Mary has taught me to use the right words to help make my conversations more efficient with my personal life, my All Star Financial family, and more importantly, how to gain trust quickly with potential clients as well as with existing clients.

Statistics show that nine out of ten conversations fail because of the words we use and how we say them. Mary helped me realize that to be as successful as I wanted to be, I needed to learn that conversations can be made or broken with a few right or wrong words. Mary taught me that in all my conversations I needed to think before speaking. Talking with my kids, grandchildren, the All Star Financial team, clients, and potential new clients should take a planned and concerted effort. I needed to practice using certain words and phrases. If I can keep the person's green light on in our conversation, I learned that I can build and rebuild trust more quickly.

Mary has worked one on one and in a series of group sessions to help the whole team at All Star Financial realize that "*words do matter.*" Her process and thoughtfulness have helped solidify a good company into a better company that is striving to go from good to better to best. In the last two years our client retention level is as high as it could be, and our growth has been unprecedented.

All of Mary's professional experiences has given her the perspective she needed to find her niche in creating trust amongst family, friends, teammates, and current as well as new clients. We are blessed to have her on our team. All Star Financial would not have the culture of listen to learn and caring what we do now without Mary's teachings. When Mary asked me if I would be interested in writing the foreword for *Make or Break Conversations* I was honored beyond words.

Mary, thank you for your time, and diligence in creating a *discipline* that works. I am proud to have been part of creating this awesome book and look forward to more financial professionals learning the words, phrases, questions, and statements that create a great conversation. *Words do matter.*

Bob Klefsaas

Founder and CEO All Star Financial, Senior Wealth Manager, CFP, AIF, CDFA

CHAPTER 1

Why High-Trust Conversations Are Your Competitive Advantage

Most financial professionals report they have no trouble talking to their clients, but the question is: are those conversations building relationships that last?

Typically, human nature is to judge ourselves as more skillful than we actually are. This is a known cognitive bias that psychologists call illusory superiority. Simply put, we tend to overestimate our positive qualities and underestimate our negative ones.

Financial professionals and their teams committed to excellence have learned a surprising truth about talking to clients: People don't just want conversations about facts, numbers, and market knowledge; they want to know that you listen and that you care.

Unfortunately, few financial professionals know how to have this kind of conversation. The purpose of this book is to examine make-or-break conversations and teach you how to listen deeply and ask questions about what really matters.

When you have the skills to masterfully lead a make-or-break conversation, you gain a powerful competitive advantage over those who just stick to the facts.

Words Have Great Power

The words that we use every day indicate how we see, hear, and value those around us. Words carry messages of whether we are included and liked or not. Being included is a primary need for all. In his book, *Social: Why Our Brains Are Wired to Connect*,[1] social psychology researcher Matt Lieberman indicates the need for connection and inclusion is stronger than the need for safety and security, because when we feel included—we feel we are seen, heard, and valued—it opens us up to sharing with each other how we view the world. Our need to reach out and connect with others is a primary driver behind our behavior.

Little everyday things we do and say in conversations open the path for us to hear what others have to say—what is really in their hearts and on their minds.

The most powerful way to build trust is through more powerful conversations. *Make Or Break Conversations* teaches guiding principles, but not by boring how-tos, robotic responses, or scripts of conversations. You will learn how to have conversations that matter in your own way.

Based on understanding the science, psychology, and human behavior behind quality conversations, you will discover that the conversations we have, the relationships we build, the actions we take, and the results we get are simply better together. We get to become the heroes in our own stories. Isn't that what we all want?

A first step on the journey is to learn about the brain chemistry of conversations, which is covered in the following chapter.

"Let's make a special effort to stop communicating with each other so we can have some conversation."

—Mark Twain

MAKE IT OR BREAK IT

Why High-Trust Conversations Are Your Competitive Advantage

1. Master the skills of make-or-break conversations so you have a powerful competitive advantage over those who just stick to the facts.
2. Understand that clients want to know that you listen and that you care.
3. Begin the journey by learning about the brain chemistry of conversations.

CHAPTER 2

Understanding The Chemistry Of Conversations

"What's wrong with them?"

That's the question that launched me on a quest to find a better way to have productive conversations.

As an educated executive leader, I frequently pondered the question of why some people are very easy to talk with and get things done, while others could not hear a word I said and would just muddle along.

When people asked what I did, the standing joke in our house was that family members would reply, "She is the most expensive babysitter I know."

There was some element of truth in that joke.

Being well equipped educationally—with a master's in psychiatric nursing, an MBA, numerous coaching certificates, and years of experience—taught me to see the world through the lens of a problem-solution framework. I knew how to create metrics, strategies, plans, and processes, and how to talk *at* people to get them on board.

"Like any workplace, we have our share of disputes, personality conflicts and bad behavior. Ideally, we're looking for an office manager with previous experience running a daycare."

And if they did not get with the program, there were two options: replace them and find someone who could do the job, or persuade them to go along.

I was not only ineffective in this approach, I was exhausted. I had heard that's the way people are; they are resistant to new ideas and change, so just keep telling them. That's why I got paid the big bucks.

About that time, the big buzzword *trust* was hitting the scene. There is a plethora of advice that says, "Here are the seven tips/tricks/techniques/scripts, and this is what you need to do." While I did not disagree with that, for me, there had to be more than those solutions.

I set out on a journey to find out what this trust thing was and how it works in building relationships so I could give up the babysitter role.

Sitting at my computer surfing the web for a different answer, I came across a new book called *Conversational Intelligence.*[2] I bought it, devoured it, and worked with its author and mentor Judith Glaser for the next three years, not only to understand it, but to put the neuroscience of conversation into practice.

I had found what I was looking for—a scientific framework and methodology with years of practical implementation behind it to finally explain what happens in the brain during conversation, and the skills required to lead these conversations and earn trust.

One might think I rushed out to teach this to my clients. Not so. Being a bit of a skeptic, I first applied this in my own life and business, and discovered people were opening up to me to talk about what was really important to them. I slowly introduced the concepts to my clients who are leaders in financial services. They would say simply, "This stuff works . . . I know how to build trust and keep that going."

There is nothing wrong with others' ability to trust; you just need to lead conversations in a different way.

Unlike other resources that focus on *this is what you do*, you must first learn how the chemistry of conversations impacts what you say, what others hear, and the actions they take. By applying the principles that make or break conversations, you can lead effective conversations that tap into the best in others.

Every conversation matters. In one moment, in one conversation, what is said or not said has the potential to make or break a relationship. Why settle for good, mediocre conversations that leave people feeling neutral and okay? You can discover how to lead better conversations that emotionally connect; you will listen deeply and ask questions about what really matters to others. They then feel safe, understood, and heard. Not only does it feel good to you, you become known as that leader or firm who listens and cares.

Examine Your Conversations

Are your conversations standing in the way of building healthy relationships that earn trust? Growing up, we were taught that conversations are about talking, sharing information, telling others what is on our minds, and telling people what to do. But conversations go deeper than sharing information; conversations are dynamic and influence—from moment to moment—the way we connect, engage, and interact with each other.

The problem is that there is not much guidance as to what constitutes a good conversation. A Stanford University study found that nine out of ten conversations miss the mark.[3] So while you may think that you are communicating well with your clients or your team as their leader, what you are trying to communicate to another person may get muddled in translation; we talk past each other, over each other, we interrupt, we trigger each other, we speak louder and gesture more. We stop listening.

What's Inside A Conversation?

Neuroscience provides insights to help us understand what goes on in the brain of every single one of us that influences our everyday conversations.

Conversations are made of up both a biochemical and an emotional reaction. In the course of a conversation, if you perceive a threat, you react with fear. Cortisol and other biochemicals are released. When you feel threatened, the thinking brain shuts down. We get the response that Daniel Goleman calls the "amygdala hijack."[4] The amygdala, part of the limbic system of the brain, alerts you that there is a perceived danger ahead. This paralyzes your brain's ability to think and moves into self-protection with a fight, flight, freeze, or appease response. In this protective mode, there is little trust in the conversation.

In a conversation where you feel safe, respected, and cared about, different biochemicals release, such as oxytocin and dopamine, that activate the executive brain. The prefrontal cortex (or, the executive brain) literally opens up and allows one to build: relationships, partnerships, empathy, good judgment, thinking ability, strategies, and innovation; handle difficult conversations; and express oneself. In this connect mode, trust develops.

But conversations are more complex than feeling trust or distrust. Trust and distrust live together in the brain and coexist in the same conversation. If we see eye to eye on things, trust develops. If we disagree or have a different point of view, there is a great degree of uncertainty in the brain. Because the limbic brain processes the perceived threat faster than the executive brain, distrust and protective behaviors occur more easily. This results in conditional trust.[5]

These biochemical shifts happen in a split second. What we say, how we say it, and what we do can make or break a conversation. You can become a trusted partner in a nanosecond but lose it just as quickly, in one conversation, in one moment, in one connection. The hidden language of trust is encoded in every conversation. By learning how verbal messages and nonverbal behaviors signal different parts of the brain and trigger certain reactions and responses, you can develop the self-management and skill to build and strengthen relationships with others, one conversation at a time.

Levels Of Conversation

Every conversation we have can either make or break a relationship. The level of conversation we use moves people into either a mode of protection or connection.

While your intentions may be positive, the impact of the conversation and the interactions that develop may not be. Every interaction we have leaves a lasting impression. The brain stores conversational patterns and interactions that influence how people will feel about talking with you in the future. Every conversation matters.

But not all conversations are equal. By understanding and mastering the impact of all three levels of conversation patterns discussed below, you can identify the context and purpose of the conversation and use them where appropriate.

You can tap into the parts of the brain that are designed for connection and bring out the best in people by consciously activating your "executive brain" instead of being run by your amygdala (in the limbic brain), which is responsible for triggering your protection response.

LEVEL ONE: Informational Conversations

"If something happens to you, your young family will struggle. There is only one way out of this. This is what you need to do."

"Here is the strategy to reach the goal of making numbers by the end of the month. You know what you each need to do. Are there any questions? If not, let's go!"

The focus is on getting facts, giving updates, telling people the strategy, and how to solve a problem. It is beneficial to confirm what you know in giving information. You may ask a few questions so you can give information that provides clear directions, set standards, and policy. Listening is limited to hearing at the word level. While you may hear the words of the other person, you are primarily aware of your own opinions, judgments, and how you will respond. These conversations are not deep and are usually in the realm of asking and telling. Informational conversations feel transactional; there is no emotional connection at this level and little trust.

The impact of this is like a monologue; you're just telling people what to do. You end up talking too much and gather only a few facts. There is a biological reason to explain this: When you express yourself, your body releases a high level of reward hormones and you feel great. The more you talk, the better you feel, which leads to talking more.

However, when you start preaching and thinking you will get buy-in, the opposite happens. The person sitting across from you cannot get a word in edgewise and feels unheard, unimportant, and marginalized. They feel as if they don't matter because you've monopolized the conversational space. They feel like a soldier who has been given marching orders. People don't like to be told what to do.

As an ambitious, driven leader, you have been taught this top-down command-and-control approach. Whether your clients or your team, because you are the expert or the boss or you know more, they go along to get along, until they don't.

Sam's Story

Sam—a driven, ambitious, smart leader known for getting things done—was given a huge project to implement in thirty days. In fact, it was a make-or-break project demonstrating he was ready for that next-level promotion into a greater leadership position.

He called his team together and clearly outlined the nonnegotiable initiative time frame. Within that short deliverable cycle, he charted what each person was responsible for, specific tasks, and how it would all come together in the end. At the first week's team meeting, some had delivered and some had not. He reinforced the plan and his expectations. The second week, he got similar, mixed results. He again focused on tasks completed and set expectations. As the deadline came closer, he started thinking, *I'm not going to mess around with those not doing the work. It's a waste of time. I have the talents and skills to do the work myself, even if it means sixteen-hour days for two weeks* (which it did).

The project went off without a technical hitch. He was proud of his accomplishment and met with his boss, feeling euphoric because he knew what it meant for him. Yet, Sam was greeted with, "The technical part was a success, but it left a trail of people not wanting to work with you and feeling really pissed at you. I am moving you to a different team, and here is the performance improvement plan you need to measure up to if you want to stay with this company." He went from promotable to PIPed.

Why? Sam did not know the limitations of Level One conversations. While Level One is useful in communicating nonnegotiable strategies and timelines, it is not effective in getting people to work well together or in figuring out how each could contribute to specific work plans.

Sam's intention was good—get the project done—but how he talked to people to accomplish this left them feeling disengaged. There was no room in the conversational interaction for other ideas, pushback, what ifs, or dialogue. People were told what to do and how to do it, and there was no room for different ideas to emerge. None of us like to be told what to do.

LEVEL TWO: Positional Conversations

Positional conversations bring understanding and clarity. You don't just tell people what to do; you ask questions about their opinions and perspectives. You give them opportunities to discuss differences and similarities openly. When we agree with the situation and solutions to move forward, we collaborate. When we agree, a win-win is created and a trusting relationship is developed. Although there is some focused listening to questions asked, there is also hesitancy to go deeper into different views and interpretations.

Herein lies the slippery slope that you may be unaware of. You are open to influence and to understand others until there is a point of view that is quite different than your own. This difference automatically triggers your brain to release cortisol as a response to this perceived threat. You try to persuade others to see your point of view and to prove your point. You go to great lengths to defend your way—the best way.

The conversation then turns into a one-person show about you—how great your firm is, how you are the top-rated expert—and then out come the charts and graphs. You are exerting power over others using your position and authority; you influence and persuade them to see things your way. You have given the presentation with all the bells and whistles, so now you expect your potential client or team to agree and buy into your recommendations. It's like telling your children to do their homework.

However, others feel uncertain if you really have their best interests at heart; they question if you were really listening. The brain senses uncertainty and creates doubt. At best, you may get compliance and conditional trust.

While others may understand your point of view, they feel like they are backed into a corner, unwilling to challenge or speak up, and not part of the conversation, and that you really had a hidden agenda all along to get them to see things your way. They feel you are not listening, you don't care, and they are just a number to you, just another cog in the wheel. Maybe they will follow through, maybe not.

If you communicate this way, you run the risk of developing relationships with people who go along to get along and bring mediocre performance results. Don't get me wrong, I'm sure they aren't waking up and jumping out of bed thinking, *How will I just get by today?* But when people don't speak up and you constantly try to convince them your way is only the right way, it can erode to mediocrity.

A Harvard study found this counterproductive silence and fear of speaking up creates teams where people waste a great deal of time and energy; the average person wastes seven days a year complaining, doing unnecessary work, and ruminating or getting angry instead of speaking up.[6]

Pat's Story

The same interaction is true with clients. *Satisfied* clients are not enough, which is a lesson Pat learned.

Know this: If you have satisfied clients and a good relationship with them, it will survive until someone else who is better comes along. You may never know why because they leave without telling you. Even if you did ask them what happened, chances are they will not tell you. The conversations you had with them created relationships where they were not engaged and invested, and you became another commodity in the marketplace.

"We have reviewed the data, and given what it shows us, you would agree that the best course of action is to implement this, wouldn't you? Here is what you need to do."

This is exactly what happened to Pat's client. They had a solid working relationship until that conversation where he knew he was right and out came the charts and graphs. While he thought he was being helpful, you can imagine how the client felt. The client left knowing the facts and the solution but feeling like the real problem was never addressed. The client never returned.

LEVEL THREE: Transformational Conversations

Transformational conversations focus on building meaning, sharing opinions, and discovering what others think and feel to create an emotional connection. When you care about what others think and feel, the brain senses safety and the prefrontal cortex opens as a signal to trust. As a result, there is an openness to share what you know with others and to discover what you don't know; you listen without judgment to the underlying mood, tone, and impact of the conversation. You are aware of the shift in energy. You listen for the essence of what they are trying to say between the lines. You listen with an openness to what is unknown and hold the conversational space for what can emerge.

The impact? Your conversations earn trust. Others feel heard and valued, and as a result, they want to work with you. The best solutions are cocreated (made together). Ideas, opinions, and different points of view are encouraged. When there are challenges, the conversation is allowed to go deeper into them and to talk them through, openly and honestly.

The interaction results in a dialogue of a healthy two-way discussion. People feel involved in the conversation, not stupid or forced to cover the truth. They know where they stand and what they can expect, as their ideas and thoughts were listened to and heard.

Michelle's Story

Michelle had the sense that there was more she could do to increase her team's performance and productivity. Together, we developed guiding principles for an upcoming staff retreat. On the day of the retreat, Michelle opened by sharing her vision for the company. And then she said something her team was not expecting: "I don't have the answers of how we do that—and that is why we are here today."

Collectively, the team had a conversation that was more open, honest, and real than any conversation they'd ever had before. From this foundation, the team took charge of creating their own agreement about how they talk to one another, addressing challenges and everyday conversations without relying on Michelle.

They identified roadblocks that were preventing them from taking action, and prioritized work for the next ninety days. They even created a tool to use during client meetings to raise the bar on client service.

Michelle's team members relate to one another differently now, because they know their ideas are heard, valued, and considered. The firm is on track to grow by 20 percent this year, without additional staff. Now, the team meets quarterly to review progress and set priorities for the next ninety days. A clear structure and place to talk through changes have decreased duplicative work and reactive, knee-jerk decision-making, while increasing innovative problem-solving.

Perhaps best of all, Michelle reports a boost to team morale. "The trust my team has created has made all the difference. We really have each other's back and figure out problems together. This is new. It's not all on my shoulders anymore."

Where do your conversations live? Benchmark Communications has studied patterns of interactions and how people communicate for thirty-five years. Its research indicates that most conversations live in Level One or Two.[7] We raise our children by telling them what they should do. We send people to school to learn how to engage in Level Two conversations, lock them into winning and success strategies, and reward them for being great at influencing others.

But when you understand how to open the space for Level Three conversations, all parts of your brain are activated. You understand how your brain influences what you think, feel, imagine, and do. Most importantly, you can choose the right level of conversation in the right context at the right time. It is this agility in talking with others that makes or breaks conversations and gives you the edge that inspires others to work with you because you have now become a trusted partner.

So, next time you sit down with your clients, staff, or coworkers, take the lead in having a Level Three conversation and build trust, loyalty, and relationships that will last a lifetime. That takes self-management. The next chapter looks at how to move from self-awareness to self-management.

MAKE IT OR BREAK IT

Understanding The Chemistry Of Conversations

1. Every conversation has both a biochemical and emotional component that influences what is said before words are spoken.
2. Understand that clients and teams want to know that you listen and that you care.
3. The level of conversation you lead either moves others into connection with you or protection from you.
4. Your agility to discern the right level of conversation, at the right time, and the right context inspires others to work with you as a trusted partner.

CHAPTER 3

From Self-Awareness To Self-Management

Spiritual author Eckhart Tolle once wrote, "Awareness is the greatest agent for change."

Having a clear sense of purpose, direction, strategy, and superior execution are important keys to success. The driver behind this is how we communicate with others. What you say and how the other person hears and responds to what you say influences your strategic and financial results.

Leaders who are self-aware, hold others accountable, and execute tough decisions in an inspiring manner ultimately drive hard results. Leaders with strong interpersonal skills deliver better financial results.

A study done by Green Peak Partners and Cornell University concluded that "results-at-all-costs" leaders actually diminish bottom-line results over time and lead to underperformance in most executive functions, while self-aware leaders with strong interpersonal skills delivered better financial performance.[8]

Self-awareness and self-management of your own emotions are probably the most important, least-discussed skills in communication. Communicating effectively begins with self-awareness. Daniel Goleman describes self-awareness as knowing your internal state, preference, and resources.[9] When we see ourselves clearly, we are more confident, more creative, we make better decisions, and build stronger relationships.

How we lead conversations is at the root of inspiring others to take action. Yet the most underdeveloped skill is moving people to action where they willingly and happily take part in the job to be done.

Everything happens though conversation. The quality of conversations you lead cause others to either to move into a mode of self-protection, fear, and shutdown, or into connection, belonging, and opening up. How we communicate determines the level of connection in our conversation. The ability to connect builds healthy relationships with a foundation of trust. Neuroscientists and psychologists consider the need of human beings to connect and belong to be more powerful than the need for safety and security.[10] In order to connect with others, we must know how what we say and do fosters or impedes that connection.

Connection Is Created Through Conversation

Most people think they are pretty good at conversations. Ever since you learned how to talk, you were in conversation. Conversations were mostly asking and telling; your parents asked you a question, and you gave an answer. Your teachers asked a question and you gave an answer. And when you were not correct, you were told what the correct answer was. Or maybe you were a bit of a rebel. When you did not get the answer you wanted, you asked other people. You learned how to effectively defend or persuade others to agree with you to see the way you thought, your point of view. You talked to share information, let others know what was on your mind, and told them what they needed to do.

We now know through neuroscience research[11] that conversations are complex. In every conversation, the chemistry of conversation is operating. This interplay of chemical and emotional activity going on in our brain influences what we hear and say. It signals connection or protection. The words you speak, how you speak them, how you listen, and nonverbal cues are the result of this chemical interplay. This is true for all humans and is a hardwired into our DNA.

While we cannot change this chemical–emotional interplay, we can learn the science and skills required to manage ourselves and to lead others in conversations that create healthy relationships. When you tap into the parts of the brain designed for connection—the executive brain—you bring out the best in people. Talking with others run by the amygdala—the limbic/primitive part of the brain—triggers the fear response.

Chemical And Emotional Interplay

The brain is mathematical, predictable, and loves certainty. Safe and secure in the experiences and knowledge you have, it stores information in your memory banks. This serves you well. With all the information coming in every day, you count on knowing what you know without having to think about it.

However, when the brain detects differences between what it knows and what is being presented, it perceives a threat and alerts you. This triggers an unexpected, intense, emotional reaction to an internal or external situation. The types of events and responses are individual and unique to the person and situation.

A triggering event causes a release of neurotransmitters in response to the threat; this is known as the amygdala hijack. The limbic brain goes on high alert, the amygdala takes over to protect you from whatever you are interpreting as dangerous or threatening. Stress hormones like cortisol are released and there is an immediate physiological reaction. You may notice a racing heart, more rapid breathing or difficulty breathing, a sensation of blood rushing through your body, flushed face, fuzzy-feeling head, a tightening of muscles, or generalized tension throughout your body.

In a split second, you react unconsciously on autopilot. If being run by the primitive brain, your brain chemistry changes and disables the executive brain from making thoughtful, rational decisions. You may go into the familiar fight, flight, freeze, or appease reaction. You *fight* to win your point and tell others how wrong they are. You go into *flight* mode to figure out how to avoid or get out of the situation pronto. You may *freeze* by shutting down and pulling away. For the moment, you *appease* by going along to get along.

The trigger impacts how you feel, how you behave, and what you say in conversations. You talk over others, you interrupt, you speak loudly to get your point across, you monopolize the conversation. In a nanosecond, you can say things that move others from feeling you are a trusted friend or advisor to someone who cannot be trusted because your words and conversations have triggered them. This is why nine out of ten conversations miss the mark.

For example, you are going about your day as usual when *it* happens. Something rubs you the wrong way, your feathers get ruffled, and your buttons are pushed.

- A colleague tells you your well-thought-out idea will not work.
- You are leading an important meeting when someone says, "Just get to the point."
- The leader asks for ideas but concludes, "We have always done it this way."
- A client dropped the ball on what he promised to do, "Because I didn't get around to it."
- Your partner announces to you, "This is what we will do."

Or maybe you had rough morning getting out of the house, tough traffic, bad weather, slow drivers, and the first person to ask you a question gets a snippy "You should know that by now."

You have been triggered and are not even be aware of it. A *Harvard Business Review* article by Tasha Eurich[12] found several consistent behaviors of individuals who are not self-aware; they will not listen or accept feedback. They cannot empathize or accept another's perspective. They have difficulty reading the room and are hurtful to others without realizing it. They take credit for success and blame others for failure.

Communicating from a place of self-awareness is the strongest predictor of overall success and a critical leadership skill. It allows you to work with others who have differing strengths and makes it easier to accept that someone else may have a better idea. Without it, it is hard to see the impact you have on others. This is why it is critical to develop self-awareness; you can guide conversations beyond your internal dialogue, tune into what others are saying, and inspire action.

The Triggering Cycle

Before you can manage your immediate reaction and move into a more thoughtful response, you must recognize your own triggers and their cycles. The cycle of a triggering conversation happens in a split second.

An emotional trigger causes you to react unexpectantly or intensely to an internal or external circumstance. It is unique to you and can be anything that creates a strong emotional reaction—people, events, situations, things, memories.

Something is said or you get a nonverbal behavior clue that does not match up with what you think, believe, have experienced, learned, or what you know to be true.

There is an automatic biochemical reaction. The amygdala hijack releases cortisol, activating the protect–fear network. Your rational, executive brain shuts down.

There is an emotional reaction: You instantly begin to recall past experiences, you jump to conclusions about others and what they are saying, and make judgments about the situation.

There is also a physical reaction as mentioned above, that you may or may not notice. It can range from being "hot under the collar" with a flushed face, rapid heartbeat, racing mind, muscle tension like a clenched jaw or an overall sense of tightness, an urgency to set the record straight, or a desire to pull away if you don't know what to say.

You disconnect from the conversation and your ability to listen to what the other person is saying. The brain cannot make sense of all that is going on, so it creates assumptions, weaves a story, or jumps to conclusions, and you say things in the heat of the moment you may later regret.

You react without a second thought about the impact your words may have. You are influenced by this internal dialogue and the conclusions you've made. Your emotions have taken over your brain. You have been triggered. You are in protection mode and on autopilot. When controlled by the amygdala, you see the world only through your point of view, which restricts your thinking and responses. You say things you may not really mean and unintentionally trigger those in conversation with you.

How about you? What are triggers that make you react on autopilot and in protection mode? Here are some examples:

- Someone cuts you off while you are making a point in a meeting or in a conversation
- You show up to a meeting on time, but only a few are there
- You keep getting interrupted trying to meet a deadline
- Others are telling you what to do and not asking for your ideas on how to do it
- Your project deadline is shortened dramatically

- You don't have the resources to do the work you are responsible for
- Your clients or team members stall in doing what they said they would
- You feel annoyed by seeing an email or voicemail from a particular person
- You are about to make a difficult phone call
- Your teenager comes home with a D on a final
- You have family members who cause disruption
- A family member is ill and you have to drop everything to make arrangements

Do you react on autopilot in less than productive ways when triggered? These statements may sound familiar to you:

- I don't even know why I said that
- I really did not mean it like that
- They just pushed me to my limit
- I was caught off guard
- I just reached the end of my rope
- I've just had it with them

The ability to identify your triggers in conversations is the precursor to the ability to self-manage how you will respond, not react. Self-awareness is noticing what is going on inside of you, around you, and tuning into the physical, emotional, and mental reactions you are having. Identifying your triggers gives you the ability to recognize what is happening to you in a conversation.

"Yes, I think I have good people skills. What kind of idiot question is that?"

Self-Awareness Is Not Enough

Translating self-awareness to self-management is the key to making or breaking conversations.

In the throes of the amygdala hijack, all you can do is react because of the brain's protective mechanism. Your reaction to triggers in conversations will break the relationship every time. Things go unsaid, assumptions are made, you tell people what to do, and you reach solutions to issues that may not be the real problem. Trust is never developed, or worse yet, unintentionally broken.

The ability to identify your triggers in conversations gives you the ability to self-manage how you will respond, not react. It requires a willingness to learn how to override and regulate your chemistry and triggers. You can interrupt your reactive patterns. You can develop an expanded view of what is going on in the conversation—the impact your conversations have on others, better ways of interacting—and healthy conversations emerge. Management of your triggers allows you to lead conversations that really matter and get to the heart of what is unsaid. When you do this, the other person feels heard, seen, and valued. This is what makes relationships and builds trust.

The ARC system supports you in managing your triggers. The implementation of awareness, responsiveness, and curiosity takes practice. The more you do it, the easier it becomes.

The ARC System

A: Awareness; Know Your Triggers. The triggered reaction is rooted in intrapersonal issues that have been unexplored or unresolved. This includes current life issues; unresolved past issues; feelings of fear, anxiety, frustration, or anger; and the need for control, to be seen as competent, and to be liked. Take note of what people, behaviors, or situations set you off. Think back over the past six months; chances are, you will identify patterns of people, phrases, or problems that do it.

R: Response Flipping. You can flip your response from a negative to a positive purpose/intention. Take responsibility for the emotional reaction to your triggers. Instead of letting this emotional reaction take over your brain and say something you will later regret, use your emotions as a warning system. While it may be easier to judge, intimidate, or put people down, recognize these negative intentions are counterproductive. If you react in this way, you may temporarily feel better because you think you are right, but it leaves the other person feeling less than, criticized, and judged because you really don't know the situation. It does not lead to a healthy relationship. When you recognize these negative intentions, you can choose a different response and shift to a more productive conversation. Some call it taking the high road, choosing to see only the best, or giving others the benefit of the doubt

C: Stay In Curiosity. Be curious by asking one more pertinent question. This shifts the conversation back to the other person and allows you a few seconds to breathe and refocus. Not just any old question will do, but an open-ended question for which you do not have the answer. This closes the gap between what you assume is going on and what is the reality of the actual event. When we open up the conversation to discovery, we bridge this gap. Others are not shut into protection and defending, but sense a caring and candor that moves the brain and the conversation into connection. The executive brain opens up and we can have a dialogue.

When I was the dean for an adult education program, we, the faculty, made special considerations for an up-and-coming student. She came to the first three classes and participated, then she stopped. Emails and phone calls were not returned.

The story we told ourselves was not pretty: she was irresponsible, she didn't care enough to return messages, she would never get the full benefit of the class, and her evaluation of the course and the instructors would be negative. And when she did come back to class, we would tell her exactly that.

Two-thirds through the course, she showed up again. But instead of focusing on assumptions and judgments, the conversation started very differently.

"I am happy you are here tonight. We have missed you and were concerned that something was going on. It is not like you to not reply to messages. How are you?"

With that simple question, the conversation opened up and the dialogue began. We learned and understood what was going on in her world. She openly shared her husband had emergency surgery and was fine now, but with all that going on, she was overwhelmed, and the last thing on her mind was class. Now that the dust had settled, she was ready to recommit to getting the most she could from the coursework and time remaining. From that dialogue, we created a plan for how we could best support her success in the time remaining.

Translating self-awareness to self-management requires you are not only aware of what is going on around you, but you tune into the physical, emotional, and mental reactions of others. Based on that awareness, you are intentional about what you say or do.

Understanding your triggers and emotional responses gives you the ability to manage them instead of letting them manage you. Embodying self-management means more than just knowing yourself; it's knowing how to master the conversation and create connection with others. Understanding what is happening in a conversation in real time—reading other people and supporting them to say what they are thinking—is the essence of connecting with others.

Knowing yourself is the foundation to knowing how to lead masterful conversations.

MAKE IT OR BREAK IT

Understanding The Chemistry Of Conversations

1. Translating self-awareness to self-management is critical to lead quality conversations.
2. Self-aware leaders with strong interpersonal communication skills deliver better financial results.
3. Identifying your emotional triggers gives you the ability to manage your response, not react.
4. The ARC system teaches the specific steps to self-manage and lead healthy conversations.

INVESTMENTS AND FINANCIAL PLANNING

"MY SHORT-TERM FINANCIAL GOAL IS TO SURVIVE UNTIL TUESDAY. MY LONG-TERM FINANCIAL GOAL IS TO SURVIVE UNTIL FRIDAY."

CHAPTER 4

Meet The Money Archetypes

In the words of the American philosopher, author, and religious scholar Jacob Needleman: "If you do not know how you are with money, you simply do not understand yourself. Period."

We all have patterns around money. These patterns are well ingrained and we may not be aware of them. Before the age of seven or so, when our brains were not developed enough to discern truth, we took in the world as everything being true. We believed what our parents, families, teachers, religious leaders, TV, and what friends told us about money. We believed in Santa, the Easter Bunny, and the Tooth Fairy. Like little sponges, we believed what we were told and experienced.

We may have had experiences with our parent losing a job or having to move because we could no longer afford the house; we did not understand the concept of money, but we did know money was the reason for our upheaval.

Stories and memories about money are stored inside of each of us. These stories and defining experiences from the past have made us who we are today and shape how we approach money. They influence, shape, and form our core identity, which is simply the person we believe we are. It represents our concerns and responsibilities in the present, different life stages, what consumes our energy, and our hopes and aspirations for the future.

Rarely do we talk about our relationship with money—how we think about it, how we feel about it, where or how we learned these patterns, what they mean to us, and how they show up. As a result, they go dormant in our memory bank, yet subconsciously influence us. It follows the idea that humans behave and make decisions emotionally, motivated and justified by logic.

Once I was sitting at the kitchen table engrossed in my favorite Sunday afternoon pleasure: reading the newspaper with the scissors right next to me as my trusted companion. I was clipping and cutting coupons to save a few cents. Secretly, I was thinking a few cents here and there would pay for the new purse in the closet I spent way too much on. But I really wanted it and it made me feel so good to show it off, no matter the price.

My husband casually approached me with a chuckle said, "You are so like your mother."

That comment hit me like a ton of bricks. He was right. Growing up, we had everything we needed, but there were those shopping trips to Dayton's with Mom to buy beautiful dresses to go out to dinner in. She would say with great delight, "We will cut a few other things so we can enjoy this."

Enter The Money Archetypes

Every one of us has a relationship with money that is complex and based on our personal experiences, but responses to money can be universally categorized. Carl Jung, the father of modern psychology, describes the psychological framework of archetypes as a pattern of thought that is derived from past experience and is present in the unconscious of the individual. Our money archetypes are not our personalities or who we are; the archetypes represent stories, beliefs, motivations, fears, and assumptions that are useful for understanding patterns of behaviors and conversations we lead around money.

Money is pervasive in our lives. We can't live with it; we can't live without it. It can bring a great sense of joy as easily as it can bring forth frustration and fear. It touches every aspect of our lives—work, career, leisure, home, family, and spiritual pursuits.

Yet, money is an uncomfortable subject for most of us. Money talk and our relationship with money serves as an emotional trigger. It limits our ability to understand ourselves and the conversations we have with our clients and team. When our relationship with money goes unnoticed and unexplored, in how we think about it, feel about it, and the decisions we make, it drives all of us a little crazy!

It happens like this: In conversation, something will be said that is different from what we know and believe; it triggers us. Science shows us when this happens, we can easily shut down, go into preaching mode, or unintentionally avoid an emotionally charged topic or any topic that is different than how we view the world.

As a financial advisor, you know the importance of thinking about the future, saving, and investing wisely. The client in front of you agrees with you on these principles, but tells you that her money goals are to be able to enjoy life, spend freely now, and worry about that other stuff later. You go into preaching mode complete with the charts and graphs, but to no avail. You missed the opportunity of exploring and understanding her specific ideas and her actions without understanding more of who she is and what is behind this money perspective.

As a CEO, you have invested in a new system to increase efficiency. After hours of training and team meetings, it does not meet your high standards. You say to yourself, *they are going to make this work no matter what*; you keep pushing because there is no way this investment will not pay off. Instead of asking what else you do not know, you push even harder to make it work.

We are complex human beings and have had many different experiences with money. The archetypes illuminate what may be true for you: The thinking and patterns around money you are not aware of. Recognizing and bringing the different patterns into alignment allows you to have a deeper understanding of yourself and the people you work with.

Developing self-awareness around your own relationship with money gives you focus, clarity, and the ability to accomplish what you want in life. When you understand your archetypes, you begin to understand your assumptions and triggers around money. Instead of judging others, you become more open to how others think, feel, and make decisions differently than you.

The more you understand, the more open and willing you can be in listening to deeply connect and understand your clients and team. That is why it is critical to understand yourself and patterns and relationship with money. So instead of derailing a potentially deep conversation because you're too nervous and uncertain to talk about the emotions behind money, you lead conversations that draw out the others so they feel understood.

While technical competency, ethical behaviors, and being an expert in your field are important, that is not enough. People buy not just what you do. They buy how good you are at being you—how good you are in personally understanding them and opening up the conversation so they can share with you their stories and experiences, sometimes for the first time. What people want most is your ability to listen and care.

Let's pull back the curtain and discover the eight archetypes.[13] As you read through the descriptions, note which archetypes may be true for you. I encourage you to approach this from a place of curiosity, not judgment, as you learn about the different archetypes. When we approach it with curiosity, we can ask the question of what was learned and how this influences our conversation.

THE ACCUMULATOR: A Penny Saved Is A Penny Earned

- Amazing at saving money and rarely carries debt
- Feels great joy and happiness saving money and watching it grow
- Careful to live below their means
- Quick to judge others on their money habits
- Spending money can cause angst; overthinks purchases or only buys on sale
- May miss out on opportunities because of the need to play it safe and secure
- Driven to save, as they never want to be financially dependent on others

THE RULER:
Hard Work Pays Off

- Has it together; systems, plans, and processes are all in place
- Decisive and knows they are building something of lasting value
- Natural leader who people want to follow
- Business and work dominate much of their time and attention
- Never think they have done enough or made enough, driving them to overwork
- Flexibility and adaptability to change course does not come easily
- Skips over success and accomplishments, as there is always more to do

THE MAVERICK:
I Am Going To Do It My Way

- Willing to take risks for the potential of big rewards
- Does not give in to the opinions of others
- Hero for the underdog by modeling what is possible
- The tried-and-true way is not exciting or something they value
- Does not like to be told what to do
- Gets caught up in the need to win approval by showing what they are made of

The Celebrity: The Only Place Is The Spotlight

- Loves to stand out in a crowd and impress people
- Loves being recognized as generous
- Has a magnetic, charismatic presence
- Their image of success does not always match the real story
- By keeping the attention on their outward appearance, they protect themselves from judgment of others
- Does not easily allow others to see their vulnerabilities and who they really are

THE ALCHEMIST: Principles And Causes Above All Else

- Visionary and idealistic in seeing what is possible
- Has a lot of ideas and the greater good is all important
- Very empathetic and empowers others to move forward
- There is a negative charge around money and never has enough
- May find themselves relying on others for financial support
- Bounces around from idea to idea and finds it challenging to see things through

THE NURTURER:
I Will Help You

- Very generously gives to others, sometimes at the sacrifice of themselves
- Appreciates money and feels the need to give more than they have
- Provides great value and service to others
- Willing to take on extra work and go beyond what is required
- Finds it easy to give unsolicited advice, which can disable people they help
- Feels resentful when others do not heed their advice

THE CONNECTOR:
Relationships Are The Most Important Thing

- Deeply cares about heart-to-heart connections
- Has faith that things will always work out
- Easily creates valuable relationships with others
- Blindly trusts others to make financial decisions for them
- Believes that somehow they will be taken care of financially
- Finds it challenging to ask people to work with them

THE ROMANTIC:

Life Is To Be Enjoyed Now; You Can't Take It With You

- Lives life to the fullest, often indulging themselves and others
- Believes life and money are to be enjoyed now
- Buys things to bring pleasure or just because they feel like it
- Often does not see the point in saving money
- Shrugs off smart money practices, telling themselves they are not good with money
- Spending can be a cover-up to avoid feelings of emptiness and worthlessness

Take a few minutes to identify what may be true for you and how those characteristics may be influencing your conversations.

1. Identify your top archetype based on what may be true for you.
2. What stories, beliefs, and experiences have influenced you and shaped your patterns around money? What do you tell yourself?

    A. What about this serves you? *When I am at my best I . . .*________________

    B. What gets in your way? *When I am not at my best I . . .* ________________

C. What do others say or do that triggers you the most? ___________________

D. How does this show up in communicating with others? ___________________

Is A Seven-Year-Old Running Your Show?

This is the question I ask financial professionals when we are together. It is provocative, I know. But it also cuts to the heart of the matter that is a universal truth: Money patterns show up in the way you think about money, handle money, and talk about money. When you do not know what your patterns are, they run your business decisions and conversations! Not good. And it's certainly not going to help you get to the next level in your business.

Did you know you have hot buttons around money? Most people, even financial advisors, don't think they do. But here is the truth: People see the world and make decision differently, especially when it comes to money. You may think you are being logical, but it is important to know there is something else running your conversations with clients.

Certain kinds of money talk may flip a switch and trigger you. Perhaps you have Accumulator patterns. Maybe you were raised by hardworking parents who taught you early on that it is important to be frugal. So, you got the message *Money is only spent when it is 100 percent necessary*.

Now, imagine sitting with a client who has a totally different approach. As your conversation goes on, she tells you how easy it is to spend money. She says things like, *Money usually seems to show up for me, and if it does not, well, life is meant to be enjoyed.*

There is a good chance this sort of relaxed attitude about money would trigger you. A lecture about the importance of saving might be on the tip of your tongue. While it would be easy to slip into talking about data on charts, graphs, and indicators (because, after all, you are the expert and could prove your point), what do you think would be the result? My best guess is that she would leave and never return. She would think, *Those financial people are all alike, they never get to the issues and listen to what I want. They just tell me what they think I should do.*

Instead, you know you have your feelings and reactions about money, spending, values, and wealth. You understand different people approach money differently and there is no right or wrong, so you stop yourself from telling her what to do. You do not give facts and figures. There is no lecturing monologue. There is no judgment. There is no staying on the surface of the conversation you lead.

Rather, you take this opportunity to get to know her on a deeper, personal level. You get curious to understand what she is thinking, what she means, and explore differences. You ask thoughtful questions to figure out how the ideas you both bring can meld together into a new and different perspective. You open up the conversation and are willing to listen to what is important to her. You care enough to give the space and time to dig deeper into challenges, fears, concerns, and stories that influenced her. You are vulnerable to share who you are as a person, where you may have tripped up along the way, and the lessons you learned. This different kind of conversation makes a relationship that lasts.

MAKE IT OR BREAK IT

The Money Archetypes

1. Money archetypes represent stories, assumptions, fears, and motivation to understand patterns of behavior and conversations you lead around money.

2. Self-awareness in your relationship with money is rarely addressed, yet it influences the quality of your conversation.

3. The archetypes illuminate patterns of how you look at and feel about money and your emotional triggers. It is critical to translate this self-awareness to self-management of your responses to lead quality conversations.

4. Understanding your relationship with money gives you the confidence to take the conversation deeper to understand the experiences of your clients and team.

CHAPTER 5

The Science Of Conversation: Introduction To Seven Principles

For the past four years, I have focused my professional speaking and executive coaching on financial CEOs, COOs, emerging leaders, and their teams. I did not plan it this way originally. One might say that it turned out to be a hidden calling.

I had several experiences with financial service professionals that left me feeling dissatisfied. In fact, I had sworn off the entire industry as one that saw me only as its next paycheck. After these experiences, I told myself I would rather take the risk of doing it myself (also known as avoidance) no matter what the downside might be, rather than put myself through another one of those relationships.

And then along came Dan. Even though he was a financial professional, I took him on as a client and justified it, since this time he was paying me. One day, he asked me to role-play as a client. I thought, *Great. Bring it on, we will see how good you really are.*

The way he was talking to me, the way he was listening to me, and the way he was guiding our conversation made me forget for a moment that this was pretend. Was he sneaky, or was he just that good at conversations? He was that good. Of course he was; I taught him! He was so good that even a skeptic like me signed up to be his client.

A Fateful Drive Home

While driving home from a social event on December 2, 2016, I was struck by the stillness of the black sky and the full moon shining so brightly that I completely got lost in the thought of the beauty before me.

Out of the clear blue, a very strange thought interrupted me. *I hope everything is okay at home.* Earlier that evening, I had given my husband a quick peck on the cheek and the dog a pat on the head and said I would see them in a couple of hours.

I walked into the house and Spy, my little Lab, who normally jumps up and down with I excitement when I come home, sauntered over to greet me. His ears were back, tail tucked between his legs.

I called out for my husband and got no response. I was a little concerned and went to the bedroom.

Whew! There he was, in bed, sleeping.

I called his name again, louder this time. Nothing.

My days as a nurse overrode my fear.

Is there breath? Nothing.

Is there a pulse? Nothing.

Is there a heartbeat? Nothing.

He was gone.

Only a few hours earlier, he was alive. Just like that, he had died.

After staying at my daughter's house for a week or so to get through the funeral stuff, the time came to go home. I turned the key and walked through the front door of my house. At that moment, it hit me really hard.

Who is left? Who can I rely on to help me figure out how the rest of this is going to work for the rest of my life?

Then I remembered I had Dan; I was not alone in this.

You are a Dan to your clients.

You become one of the most important people in their lives. It is not the future planning. It is now. They will know that they are never alone. You are there for them, to comfort them and care for them. That is what you do. You listen to learn and earn their trust.

That unlikely event brought new meaning and fresh eyes to what I now do. What I did not know then that I know now is that the wisdom and expertise you have as a financial professional to guide conversations and provide support in making decisions lasts a lifetime and changes lives forever. You make a difference.

It all started with the focus on financial professionals, and remains my first love. As the impact of the chemistry of conversation grows, leaders from other industries, such as healthcare, nonprofits, and IT, have also come into the fold wanting to learn how to build relationships, create a culture of trust, and converse so others will listen. Whether you are an executive, a financial service leader, or an emerging leader, these principles and skills are foundational to leading healthy conversations.

The single biggest challenge in life is the missed opportunity of creating meaningful conversations that build caring human relationships. Everything begins with a conversation. Without this, teams fail, profitability fails, clients leave, employees leave, parents fail, relationships fail. The quality of conversations you lead determines the quality of relationships you build.

As we learn how to have better conversations, we become better—better business leaders to our clients, teams, and colleagues. We become better in our families as partners and parents.

Conventional wisdom says conversations are for sharing information—getting to know others a little bit better so they know, like, and trust you. Then, get down to the facts. You understand the problem they have. You explain to them what you can do for them, the process, and your credentials with the goal of every conversation leading to the next one. There is very little meaning or personal connection in this typical tip-of-the-iceberg conversation.

Conventional wisdom has conversations upside down. There is so much more to conversations than what we think we see or hear. Conversations are a complex web of action and interaction. These interactions involve words that trigger biochemical and emotional reactions in our nervous system, influencing the words we use, how we speak to each other, and why we say what we do. They influence whether we can connect and lead healthy, trusting conversations or disconnect with fear, caution, worry, and distrust.

There is little guidance as to what constitutes a good conversation. While we may think we are pretty good at conversation, research indicates otherwise. The Stanford study previously mentioned revealed that nine out of ten conversations miss the mark. We are so busy thinking about what *we* will say next that we cannot listen. We talk to get our point across, raise our voice, get excited and gesture, interrupt, and keep talking *at* people. The more we talk, the better we feel, so we keep talking. We talk past each other, we talk over each other, and then we stop listening.

This book explores what really goes on inside a conversation. It teaches the chemistry of conversation based on research from neuroscience, psychology, and human behaviors. Based on forty years of research with a worldwide team of neuroscientists, this groundbreaking work of the Neuroscience of Conversation® was pioneered by my mentor Judith Glaser.

It allows us to peak inside the brain to see what is happening during a conversation. Knowing this allows us to have meaningful conversations. Conversations that go beyond the facts. Conversations that create a sense of personal connection, a space and openness to share, and safety to discover what we really do not know.

Bob's Story

Several years back, I was working as an executive coach and professional speaker teaching the chemistry of conversations to business leaders. Then, along came Bob Klefsaas. We met through a mutual friend. Bob is the CEO of a healthy wealth management firm, All Star Financial. He modestly described it as having about $2 billion of assets under management in various forms. Before it was even a thought in the financial world thirty-three years ago, he developed his business with the motto of "doing the right thing" for the people he served. That meant fee-based holistic planning customized to the individual.

I was skeptical about working with him at first. But Bob was different. He thought he was pretty good at conversations and connecting with his clients, but he was open and willing to learn how to become even better. When we started working together, I knew deep down inside if I could help him bridge the gap between how he talked to people and how they felt heard, seen, and valued, not only would his business continue to grow, but he and his firm would influence current clients and generations to come.

The results were so astounding to Bob that we worked with the entire All Star team and developed what is now called the Conversational Edge Immersion Program. Today, we have cocreated a partnership that celebrates bringing our talents together to teach leaders, top performers, and emerging professionals how to lead conversations that bring out the best in people they work with.

How It Works

Implementing this cutting-edge methodology incorporates the chemistry of conversations and skills in how we talk with each other. As a result, conversations with clients, staff, and even families build trust easily, ethically, and with integrity. It changes the way you define yourself; you see what is possible one conversation at a time. When you listen to learn, you will earn trust. It all begins with the quality of conversation you lead.

Seven principles guide the development of healthy conversations by demonstrating the impact of how what we say influences relationships built on trust. Each principle has specific conversational skills to practice and implement in your own way and in your own authentic voice.

Even in a well-established relationship, a single conversation can make or break trust in seconds. When the science, principles, and skills are applied, it give you the confidence to lead a different kind of conversation—one that comes from an understanding of how humans connect with one another.

Who It Is For, And Why Should They Care?

Trust is a hot topic. Building trust is one of the greatest challenges facing any industry. Particularly in the financial service industry, building trust is critical to everything you do.

There is a plethora of articles that tell how to communicate for creating trust, but these only scratch the surface and do not get down to the core issue.

Healthy conversations are the secret sauce to building high trust relationships.

Any conversation can break trust, or can make for superior client communication, which results in trust, engagement, a positive experience, and relationships that last. To lead these kinds of conversations, you must know what goes on inside of every conversation, the invisible chemical and emotional responses we all have, and the skills to bring out the best in people in how you talk with them.

Enormous amounts of time, energy, money, and priorities are given to developing technical expertise, process-driven systems, sales, and marketing. While these are important, fewer resources are available on how to effectively communicate this. This is based on the assumption that we all know how to talk to people; it is a basic "soft skill." Yet, it is this soft skill that drives bottom-line results.

Top performers search for ways to better serve the people they work with. They want to be the best they can be and live their calling to help people and make a difference.

The book is written for the high-performing leader, CEO, COO, wealth advisor, and emerging advisor who wants to take conversations to a new level of connectedness, but is not clear on how to get there. Does the following describe you?

- You are driven. You are open to be the best you can at human relationships.
- You care. Your profession allows you to serve. You do the right thing.
- You understand the value you bring (beyond the technical) in guiding conversations and building partnerships with others so they can talk about what is really on their minds.
- You know the best actions your clients and team can take result from deep conversations that connect, bond, and build trust with relationships that last.
- You are willing to go beyond collaboration into learning how to cocreate conversations where people have a sense of belonging and a role in making plans that you grow and implement together.
- You are open and willing to experiment with leading a different kind of conversation.

MAKE IT OR BREAK IT

The Science of Conversation: Introduction To Seven Principles

1. One of the greatest opportunities in business is building trust.

2. The key to buidling trust is knowing how to lead healthy conversations.

3. The seven principles guide how to develop healthy conversations that beget trust:

   Principle #1: Share The Air

   Principle #2: Respect Others' Opinions

   Principle #3: Stretch Thinking

   Principle #4: Discover Ideas

   Principle #5: Explore Meaning

   Principle #6: Speak Up

   Principle #7: Success Together

   Each principle is explored in-depth in the chapters that follow.

CHAPTER 6

Principle #1: Share The Air

Human beings thrive on belonging. Whether with friends, family, colleagues, clients, a religion, or something else, humans need to belong and be an important part of something that is bigger than themselves. It is through conversations we determine the feeling of belonging.

Social psychologists Baumeister and Leary[14] identified that the quality of interactions is more important than the quantity of interactions. Belonging is created by positive interaction, knowing there is a mutual concern, and others love us and care about our well-being.

Whether it's a one-to-one relationship or being part of a larger group, we all have a need to belong. And it's not just kid stuff.

In high school, I wanted to be part of the "in" group of cheerleaders because, after all, they were the popular girls, the ones who got recognized and got to perform regularly in front of the whole school. I remember the day of the tryouts. I had the physical ability to do the jumps, twirls, and splits. I was not voted to be part of the squad, but I could get over that. What I could not get over was my friends who *did* make the team turned into an exclusive group. They had private conversations and ate lunch together, saying, "This is a meeting just for us." I wanted to be part of that inner circle, part of their conversations, part of their world. I did not fit; I did not belong. And I *so* wanted that.

I learned that whether you are a kid or an adult, the need to belong and be part of something bigger than you is an innate human emotion and drive. Amy Edmondson and Kathryn Roloff concluded that people in organizations and on teams have a strong preference for others perceived to be in the "in" group and a bias against those in the "out" group.[15] We prefer others who are similar in values, attitudes, and beliefs. The quality of our communication can therefore be narrow in scope and less useful in accomplishing goals.

Fulfilling the need to belong begins with being included in conversation. People want a seat at the table. They want to know where they fit, where they belong, and that they are valued as a person for their own thoughts and ideas even if they are not on the cheerleading squad.

To address this challenge, we can incorporate the chemistry of conversation to understand what goes on in the brain so we can share the air, the conversational space, and invite others to be a part of the conversation.

Healthy conversations are foundational to healthy relationships that create trust. Many times, the language we use, the nonverbal cues, and the interactions we lead unintentionally leave others feeling that what they say does not matter, they do not matter, and they are not part of the conversation. What you say, the words you use, and how you talk with others, makes or breaks a conversation and the relationships that develop.

Back To The Chemistry Of Conversation

Our primitive brain, the amygdala, is on constant alert below the level of our awareness, monitoring for signs of danger or threats. Our survival used to depend on this. In today's world, is it unlikely that a tiger is going to eat you, but your brain does not know this. What your brain picks up through this constant scanning is that something presented is different than what you know to be true.

In conversations, if something is communicated through words, tone of voice, and/or body language that is different than how you see the world, it is translated to fear and threat. Your brain automatically notices this difference and puts you on high alert—the amygdala hijack. Your brain becomes flooded with cortisol and other neurotransmitters and it controls what you say from a fear-based, threatened position. It influences the ability to stay focused and listen to others in conversation.

The cumulative effect is that the conversation becomes run by the amygdala and contributes to why nine out of ten conversations miss the mark. We talk over each other, raise our voices, try to control the conversation, and don't listen to the other person. What was meant to be a dialogue turns into a monologue based on what we think should happen, closing down the space for others to be a part of the conversation.

In conversations where there is similarity in thought and ideas, and no feeling of threat, the response is very different. The brain is flooded with oxytocin and other positive neurotransmitters. Oxytocin is known as the bonding chemical between mother and child, and is the bonding chemical between human beings in conversation. Oxytocin opens up the prefrontal brain, allowing connection, sharing, and trust.

Conversations trigger chemical and emotional changes in the brain. These minute-by-minute chemical reactions drive how we communicate and how we develop healthy relationships. Conversations in which we do most of the talking and telling others what to do breaks a relationship, as others feel there is no space for them to contribute. But when we allow others to contribute, share opinion and ideas, open up, and partner with each other, we build trust with others and develop healthy relationships.

The solution to leading conversations that allow for a partnership to grow and develop lies in cocreating conversations.

What Is Cocreation?

I was first introduced to the idea of being in action together—being coactive—through my coach's leadership training. We are and have the ability to be creative and resourceful. When we bring these abilities and interrelations to the forefront, we share in the journey and shape our worlds together.

Cocreation in the business world began as an economic strategy to bring together customers, clients, and other relevant parties to produce a mutually valuable outcome. It is both a process and discipline to blend and bring forth new ideas, products, or services with the end user in mind.

Applying this to conversations means we work together with others for mutual benefit, support, and value. A partnership is developed so we listen without judgment, share ideas, and develop actions together.

Simply put, in cocreating conversations, we are better together. Through conversations where the air is shared, I include you and you include me; we become better together. It's beyond collaboration where you do your thing and I do mine and it may work out if we both see things the same way. It is the best of our thinking, including similar and different perspectives, thoughts, and ideas that are melded into one idea, action, or strategy. We both have a part. What is made together, stays together.

How To Share The Air

Conversational space is created so people can contribute, and know they will be included, understood, and valued for what they bring to the table. The first condition that must be established in every conversation is psychological safety.

Amy Edmondson introduced this concept, defining psychological safety as a sense of confidence that team members will not embarrass, reject, or punish someone for speaking up.[16] People who feel psychologically safe learn from their mistakes, are more innovative, and are motivated to improve their team and company.

What Does It Mean To Create Safety?

It is more than a one-time event of hanging out the "All Are Welcome Here" sign. The everyday conversations you lead are foundational in creating safety and inclusion. It happens as you work alongside others and how you communicate with them. To feel safe, others need to know they are included in the conversation and you will really listen to what they have to say, even when their thoughts and ideas are different than prevailing group attitudes; this different point of view will be acknowledged and received. Language, nonverbal cues, and subtle interactions can communicate signals of exclusion. If you are not actively including, you might be accidently excluding.

Using Conversational Shifters

Sharing the air includes others in the conversation, creating an emotional connection where they feel they belong and are safe to open up and share what they are really thinking. They are called conversational shifters, as they shift the conversational dynamics from fear, protection, and disconnection to safety, knowing they belong at the conversational table and are connected.

1. **Open your conversation with an emotional connection.** Rather than wasting these first few precious moments with weather conditions, baseball scores, or unimportant trivia, use the first moment of contact to let the other person feel that you welcome them. It calms fear, quells anxiety, and triggers oxytocin. It simply feels good. It sets the stage for openness, honesty, and sharing, for you and the other person. By your words, show you are genuinely interested in them before launching into the business you are meeting about.

   Break a conversation:

   Nice day out there, huh?

   Traffic is terrible isn't it?

   Great game last night. Did you watch it?

   We're both busy people, so let's get right to it; we have a lot to cover.

   Make a conversation:

With a warm, sincere smile, while looking into their eyes, say:

I am happy we can share this time together.

I am happy to see you.

I have been thinking about you. How are you?

Before we get started, let's take a minute to catch up. What's new in your world? Anything exciting going on? How is your family?

Remember Bob? He was skeptical that something so simple could be so powerful but he was willing to try. He now opens every conversation with an emotional connection because it triggers people into a receptive place. We have nicknamed this the million-dollar statement—something as simple as, "I am happy to see you today. How are you?"—because it has resulted in his clients investing millions of dollars with his company. Why? Because he takes the time to make a personal connection and develop a relationship before he gets into the problem. (In fact, I often tell the story of the $25 million briefcase. Bob took his time to make a relationship and personal connection and the client asked him to help her with a briefcase that contained $25 million in investable assets.)

2. **Set the context of the conversation.** Be clear about the purpose or intention of the conversation and what you want as its result. Our brains love roadmaps because they calm anxiety and create a sense of knowing what to expect and where we are going. Share your roadmap agenda so you can address what is important, what matters to you both, and how you can get there together.

3. **Have a loosely held agenda.** If other, more pressing or critical topics come up, be flexible and address those instead of skipping over or ignoring them because they didn't fit your agenda.

Break a conversation:

Come to my office; we need to talk.

Your appointment is on such-and-such a date.

Make a conversation:

Come to my office at 2 p.m. so we can review the progress we are making.

What is important to you that we talk about today? Then share what you have for the meeting, and always make space for what matters to them.

4. **Share the conversational space.** Stop talking; give others a chance to talk, and listen to what is said. This reduces uncertainty and gives the clear message that what they have to say matters. Monitor yourself and discern where to use the different levels of conversation. (See chapter 7.) If you talk too much, they cannot listen, let alone get a word in edgewise.

Break a conversation:

I will tell you the details later, but for now, what you need to do is this.

You know what to do, right?

Make a conversation:

I want to hear your opinion. (I will share mine, but first I want to hear what you think.)

How did you come up with this idea?

I noticed you have been quiet. What are you thinking? What questions come to mind?

Give them time and space to think. Be okay with silence before you jump in. Ask everyone in the room for their opinions. Tactfully call on those who aren't speaking up; they may be silent for fear of looking dumb, incompetent, or think they should know something already, but others probably have the same question.

5. **Employ transparency.** Share information and what is on your mind freely; this allows others to know what you know or don't know. They will not have to guess or feel uncertain. We all want to be "in the know." There are no right or wrong thoughts, just different points of view and beliefs.

   Break a conversation:

   Give incomplete information.

   Lack clarity and candor on what you cannot say and why.

   The next step is... and this should be accomplished by [date].

   When the decision is reached, I will share this information with you.

   Make a conversation:

   Set clear boundaries on decision-making.

   This is what you will do, and this is what I will do. What questions do you have?

   Your ideas about different options were very enlightening. Tell me more.

   I have a different opinion; may I share it with you?

   Be honest that you may not know the answer to a question, but will research it and get back to them within a reasonable timeframe.

Human beings thrive on belonging; fulfilling that need begins with inclusion. We all want to know where we fit, where we belong, and that we are valued as a person for our thoughts and ideas. Showing others respect by how we listen and respond in our conversations with them builds trusting relationships. The next chapter will address this principle.

MAKE IT OR BREAK IT

Principle #1: Share The Air

1. Open your conversation with an emotional connection. If you are not actively including others, you may be accidentally excluding them.
2. Cocreate the agenda and context of the conversation with clients and team.
3. Have a loosely held agenda and be adapatable to situations that come up that may not be on your agenda.
4. Share the conversational space. Encourage others to contribute by asking what they are thinking.
5. Assume everyone you will ever meet knows something you don't.
6. Employ transparency, even when you may not have the answer.

CHAPTER 7

Principle #2: Respect Others' Opinions

The sincerest form of respect is listening to what another has to say. Human beings thrive on learning, contributing, voicing their point of view, and thinking through challenges when they are heard. They will get behind ideas and recommendations when they feel respected and have been heard in the conversation. Without respect, there is no trust. When there is no trust, we lose our voice.

The second principle in the chemistry of conversation explains what gets in the way of really hearing someone and how you can listen differently, even when their opinions and ideas are different than yours. You can engage them in conversation rather than telling, selling, persuading, or influencing them to your point of view. Masterful conversations result when you listen to hear and respond respectfully in the moment.

You Can Open Them Up Or Close Them Down

What we say—even unintentionally—either makes a conversation that opens up another person to connect with us, or breaks a conversation that closes them down and moves them into protection mode.

In conversations where people feel heard, listened to, and recognized, they feel respected, accepted, and appreciated. This activates oxytocin, the bonding chemical, making them feel safe and open to trust. The executive brain then has access to wisdom, insight, integrity, and innovation.

Conversations where thoughts, opinions, ideas, or feelings are not heard lead us to feel rejected, disrespected, ignored, or judged. This triggers fear and distrust networks in our brain. Cortisol is activated and leads to overpowering uncertainty.

What makes this so interesting is that our brain is constantly moving back and forth in conversation based on what is said, how it is said, and the nonverbal cues given.

In conversations where you are feeling challenged, uncertain of what to say, frustrated, impatient, angry, or stressed, you are triggered into protective behaviors that impact what you say and how you listen. You cannot hear.

Protecting behavior leads to conversations where you may:

- Talk over others and interrupt
- Tell others what to do
- Judge ideas and people as right or wrong, as competent or incompetent
- Criticize or blame others for not knowing or thinking through things
- Believe that your way is the only way

The person on the receiving end of this conversation feels defensive, overwhelmed, and impotent since they are not given a chance to participate. There is nothing more powerful than feeling rejected, disrespected, or frustrated. It activates our fear network and cortisol and we shut down.

Leading conversations that move people to want to listen to us and cocreate a partnership requires us to expand our conversational patterns and skills. There is nothing more influential in elevating intelligence, personalities, skills, and decisions than healthy conversations.

The quality of your listening and your patterns of communication impact what your clients and team hear and feel. It impacts your success, your team's success, and your client engagement.

An MIT study showed that 50 percent of the difference between low-performing and high-performing teams was the quality of conversations.[17] Sandy Pentland, the head of the MIT's media lab, found that patterns of communication were not only the most important predictor of a team's success, they were as significant as **all** other factors combined, including individual intelligence, personality, and skill.

When leaders don't listen, their team or clients feel discounted and disrespected, like outsiders looking in. This elevates cortisol and reduces the ability to engage in productive conversations. People who can listen to different opinions, and move conversations into discovery with respect rather than criticism and judgment, will be successful and create solutions and innovations that were never thought possible.

Quality conversations impact each client's engagement with you. To lead meaningful conversations, you must listen to deeply to discover their unique situation, what they really want, and a personalized understanding of them. This opens up the brain and they feel an emotional connection with you, which is bigger and deeper than the financial strategies you discuss. They feel the alignment between their decisions, your solutions, and what personally matters to them.

Quality conversations where clients are heard are critical. It is foundational to personal relationships, client engagement, and providing exceptional service. The 2019 research done by Investments and Wealth Institute[18] found that high net worth investors rated foundational requirements in their advisors as being important: being trustworthy, having high ethical standards and acting in their best interests, and being knowledgeable. Beyond this foundational expertise, the drivers for the engaged clients were taking a personalized approach, demonstrating advanced capabilities, delivering exceptional service, and providing meaningful guidance.

Everything you do begins with a quality conversation. Clients cannot be heard, their priorities cannot be met, and they will not be engaged with you if you don't listen.

Why Don't We Listen?

Patterns of listening are the most important predictors of success. Whether your role is in sales, engineering, support, or as the CEO, listening is your basic tool to gather information, assess relevant information, make effective and timely decisions, and effectively connect with the people you work with.

Listening should be quite easy. You say something, I hear you. I say something, you hear me. But while we may be listening, we are not hearing.

Why is listening, that seems so simple, so complex? Two reasons: one physiological and the second emotional.

The physiological reason. The human brain is capable of processing words at a much higher speed than a person is able to speak. The average rate of speech for an American is about 125 words per minute, yet the brain processes about 800 words per minute.[19] So while the speakers' words enter our brain at a slow speed, we continue to think at a high speed.

We drop out of conversations every twelve to eighteen seconds. We get internally distracted and think of other things while the speaker is speaking. We are busy trying to evaluate the situation, jump ahead to solve the problem, compare what they are saying to our past experience, or simply take a mental sidetrack unrelated to the conversation at hand.

This results in an invisible three-way conversation. The brain is never blank; it is always thinking about something. This constant chatter, your internal dialog, is always running as an automatic response, whether you are aware of it or not.

This internal dialog is your own filter and how you view the world. It is influenced by past events, experiences, and relationships, as well as physical and emotional states, such as being tired, stressed, or frustrated. It becomes a listening stealer as it derails us from listening as we are occupied with what we are thinking about. And wait, it gets even better!

The emotional reason. When the speaker says something that is contrary to how we see the world, the inner dialog is activated by the amygdala to protect your point of view. In this emotional response, your thoughts are consumed with being right and proving their ideas are wrong. You go into interpreting, analyzing, and judging why this is not right, and the focus becomes you and what you will say next to correct or reject what they are saying.

We have disconnected from the conversation and from listening.

Levels Of Listening

What is good listening? We have been taught that it boils down to a few fundamentals.

- Give your attention to the other person.
- Do not interrupt or talk when others are speaking.
- Let others know you are listening through nonverbal expressions: lean in but not too much, make good eye contact but don't stare them down, smile politely.
- Verbally encourage others with an *uh huh*, or repeat back what has been said, like a parrot, word for word.

While these behaviors might be useful, they fall short of outstanding listening skills. To become a better listener and really hear what the other person is saying—not what you think they are saying or what you want to hear—let's explore the levels of listening.

Level One Listening—Internal Listening: As you listen, your mind is focused on your own experiences, opinions, and judgments. You pretend to be listening while thinking your own thoughts. It is surface listening; you hear the facts based on your interpretations. You do not really understand the emotions, context, or unique situation of the one speaking. Level One listening easily leads to Level One conversations: not being open to dialogue, giving advice, and telling people what to do. The impact is the other person feels defensive, disrespected, and pushed away, and no trust is established.

Level Two Listening—Focused Listening: Your focus and attention is on the speaker and you are aware of the verbal message. Trying to be a good listener, you are interested in others, yet cautious about reaching out. However, you can get defensive when criticized or when different opinions are expressed. This easily slips into Level Two conversations: using position and expertise to convince others to agree with you and maintain the status quo. The impact is the other person receives mixed messages, and there is tension and uncertainty around any respect and trust.

Level Three Listening—Global Listening: You use all your senses to feel what is happening in the moment, endeavouring to read between the lines of what others say and what is important to them. You also ask exploratory questions to support the other person in saying what they may be thinking. This leads to a Level Three conversation: the other person feels respected, valued, safe to open up, that you are on their side, and willing and delighted to engage. They begin to trust you.

Listening is not an end, but part of the interactional pattern of conversations. When we lead listening conversations, there is a chemical shift in the brain. This shift allows us to listen to connect instead of listening to figure out what to say next, how to fit into the conversation, or to correct somebody.

The more we can connect with others, the more we feel respected.

Listen To Connect

People thrive on connection and respect, not criticism and judgment. Listening to connect is the conversational skill that supports respecting others' opinions, thoughts, and ideas.

We all make snap judgments. Within a tenth of a second of seeing someone's face, we form opinions of them—even though we have not spoken a word with them. It seems that we are hardwired to draw assumptions in a fast, unreflective way.[20] These snap judgments translate to whether we see them as friend or foe. This hinders us in our willingness to listen, connect, understand, and have empathy for others.

We can manage these snap judgements and well-ingrained patterns of how we listen by learning and applying the skills of listening to connect.

Listening to connect is focusing your attention on the other person, not you. It's *let me listen to you.* You acknowledge what they have said and what that means to them before you express your ideas, thoughts, or opinions.

Listening to connect is uncovering both facts and feelings. Facts are useful and necessary to provide an orientation to a situation. We also listen for the underlying emotions in how they describe the situation, their thought process, and the impact of this and how they relate to the situation.

Listening to connect is being curious, not judgmental, about the opinions of others, their thinking, how they operate, how they see the world. In curiosity, we are open and close our own filters of information that does not conform to what we want to hear. We can ditch our mental checklist of what is important to us and what we need to and explore what is important to them.

Listening to connect is being interested in what the other person needs to say, not what we want from the conversation. We need to be clear on the purpose of the conversation, but still flexible enough to create the conversational space for what the other needs to say or contribute.

Conversational Shifts That Make Or Break Listening To Connect

Breaks: Listening for the facts to confirm what we think we already know. The conversation sounds like an interrogation. We ask for specifics so we can verify for ourselves that we understand the whole picture. We miss the important bigger picture of how they relate to the situation, what they are hoping to accomplish, and how they experience and feel about a situation—which is often more telling than the facts.

Makes: Keeping an open mind to wanting to learn about the other. We have a willingness to discover what they are trying to convey, the meaning to them of the words they are using, the body language we observe, the energy they are portraying, and the emotions they are feeling.

Breaks: We assume and guess we know what they are trying to say. Our listening stays at the surface level. We skip over subtle hints about what the speaker means and what we think they mean. We are not aware of cultural factors, the emotional state, interpersonal stressors, and anything else that constitutes the "elephant in the room."

Makes: We assume there is something to be learned from every conversation. With openness, we are better able to notice what is said and unsaid. It's paying attention to the clues the other person drops and nudging them further to talk. If we don't understand, we ask again to really understand. We need to be brave enough to say what needs to be said. If we don't, the other person feels like the conversation was a waste of time and that you really didn't listen, care, or respect them enough to go deeper.

There is never a more important time for financial advisors to listen than during or after a crisis. For instance, the COVID-19 pandemic required advisors to listen to what clients needed and determine how to support them through the significant and daily changes in their lives and businesses.

Investment and Wealth Management Institute partnered with Absolute Engagement to survey high net worth investors on how that crisis impacted client loyalty. The 2020 Special Report describes that while satisfaction with their advisor remained strong, more investors were questioning the relationship they had with their advisor and if the advisor was providing the advice and guidance they needed, and putting their needs first when making recommendations.[21]

When you are focused on communicating to your clients in uncertain times, the opportunity is there to ask if your conversations are focused on your client and you are deeply listening to connect to what concerns them. It will give you a deeper understanding of the real challenges your clients are facing. You can lead conversations and respond with clarity and meaningful guidance and support that reflects the client's needs that go beyond investments and planning.

A *Harvard Business Review* article by Zenger and Folkman summarized characteristics outstanding listeners share.[22] They ask questions to promote discovery and insight and signal they care enough to want to hear more. They make other people feel supported and safe to talk about issues and differences openly. The flow of conversation is cooperative; they aren't listening to find errors, preparing a rebuttal, or trying to win an argument. Finally, they provide feedback and suggestions, and don't jump in to solve a problem.

It takes courage to listen to connect—having the heart and inner strength for deeper listening to understand the words they use and find clues and put words to discover the real meaning behind their words. Listening to connect is not only respectful; it pulls people together in a shared bond and deeper understanding. It supports us in developing, strengthening, and making partnerships that last.

MAKE IT OR BREAK IT

Principle #2: Respect Others' Opinions

1. Make the decision that the person in front of you is the most important job you have in the moment. Commit to your purpose of the conversation: to listen to them and tune out the rest of the distractions, both physical and mental.

2. Listen for facts and emotions. Ask your clients specifically about what they think and feel in a constructive, noncritical way.

3. Support, convey confidence, and give permission to your clients to share challenges and difficulties in their life.

4. Listen from curiosity and nonjudgmentally to their point of view to explore what that means to them rather than jumping to conclusions.

5. Make suggestions and provide feedback for alternative paths instead of telling your clients what to do.

6. Listen to what is said and not said. It is more important to understand and get it right than be right.

CHAPTER 8

Principle #3: Stretch Thinking

The graduating preschool class of twenty beautiful five-year-olds sporting handmade gold banners took the podium, one by one, to tell the audience what they wanted to be when they grew up. Some were typical occupations like fireman, teacher, soccer player, and ballerina. Some were humorous: an NBA player, president of the United States, and to be really rich, which, of course, got a laugh from the parents. One little girl announced that she wanted to be kind. There was dead silence, people looking around as if to say, "What did she just say . . . *kind*?" then applause. I thought that was very interesting.

After the program, I shared with her that I loved her answer and asked why she chose kindness. Looking very intensely at me with her beautiful blue eyes, she responded, "We all can be kind." But I wanted more of her wisdom and asked what that meant. With a very matter-of-fact expression on her face, she said, "We always ask others to eat with us and play with us. We are a family."

I pondered her response. Its simplicity was very powerful. We all have a sense of what we want to be. We define this as our profession, our roles, and what we do. We also have a sense of how we want to show up as we grow up. It is what makes our everyday life meaningful. Humans all have a desire to be or become someone who is bigger or better than what they are today. It is a dream, hope, and desire we hold personally. Aspirations come in many shapes and forms, such as social, career, or personal. We all aspire to be or become something that is different or better than what we currently have. We all have aspirations. Even a five-year-old has aspirations.

Many times, we are not consciously aware of our aspirations, but they are what keeps us aiming for something higher and better. Reaching for the stars or looking and moving upward—it is what makes our everyday life meaningful and opens the door to possibilities.

Aspirations answer the question *why*. They require us to answer the questions of why we work, play, and have the relationships we do. Aspirations shine a light on the journey we take as humans in growing and developing. Aspirations drive our decisions and actions.

We don't give much attention to aspirations in everyday conversations. The focus is on the immediate problem–solution and get-into-action thinking. Occasionally, we may ask others about goals, plans, or where they want to be in a few years, then respond, "That's nice" and proceed without asking how they are going to get there.

What I learned from that five-year-old in a brief conversation is that when we create the conversational space that encourages others to stretch their thinking beyond the status quo and what they already know, a whole new realm of possibilities come to life.

When the doors of possibility are opened, we can connect the dots between what people are doing today with what they really want and what it means to get there. It allows us us to connect the dots between the work they do and understand how we can support them to nurture and grow their talents and abilities. When we ask questions, we discover it is not just the job, role, or career. It is bigger than that.

How about you? Do your conversations encourage *stretch thinking* to get to know people more deeply? When you understand their hopes and dreams, aspirations, and what is possible for them, not only do you emotionally connect with them, you have a roadmap on how you can support them in reaching for their aspirations.

Matt is a very successful wealth advisor. His client was considering retirement. Having saved and invested wisely, she had the resources available to make that decision, but felt uncertain about the timing. Matt had heard this same uncertainty with his clients many times before. He knew it was not about the money; the bigger question was what that could mean for her. He asked one question: "What are your aspirations?" The response was truly heartfelt and unexpected. It was not that long-awaited vacation or to buy something he thought she had always dreamed of. She wanted to have sleepovers with her grandchildren and not be chained to a work schedule. Further, she wanted get a riding lawn mower for her acre lot and mow it whenever she wanted, not just on days off when it didn't rain. By tuning into her aspirations and supporting her to verbalize them, she discovered clarity for herself in what was possible and options that were available to her.

Whether big or small, we all have aspirations. We can encourage and support others to articulate their world of possibilities that matter to them. Clear aspirations are the foundation of future decisions, actions, and plans.

Human beings thrive on exploring, imagining, and talking about what may be possible, unleashing the greatness inside them. All too often, we fall into focusing on the past. While that has its place, it is not a substitute for finding the right time and place to talk about aspiration and ambitions, hopes, and dreams of what could be.

Dialogue that opens up thinking about *what could be* gives leaders critical inside information about the people they work with and the opportunity to design potential growth and development opportunities beyond daily duties.

Dave's Story

My client Dave is an expert computer architect, but he wanted to contribute more than just the technical expertise his current position required. His skill set is in high demand and he knew he could move into other positions outside the company, and in fact, had several offers to do so. After much thought, he concluded that what he really wanted was the opportunity to influence his current company into something bigger. He knew it was good, but it could be better.

He shared with his CEO that while he consulted with others informally, he would like the opportunity for more formal consultation work. He had the aspiration to use both his expertise and interpersonal skills to influence and guide teams to develop cutting-edge solutions. When the opportunity came up, the CEO allowed Dave to do it. Six months into it, Dave was promoted to the leadership position of technology director, overseeing the development of four teams.

Dave understood that a basic human need is to grow and develop. It was important for him to grow into a promotion. He also understood that not everyone wants that, but they still want to grow. He used the skills in developing himself, and applying his new conversational skills, with the individuals on the team. Dave asked his team members about their aspirations. He learned how they wanted to grow and contribute. Some wanted to develop new ideas, some wanted to contribute by following the plan. Based on his understanding of aspirations, talents, skills, and abilities, he developed a complementary mix of teams that supported people where they were and stretched them to grow.

In working with the teams, Dave knew about the "past trap." Conversations can easily focus on, "This is what we have done in the past, this is what worked well, and this is what we need to improve upon." The work gets done, the projects get completed, and a few new ideas may be implemented. However, the opportunity to grow and develop something better is missed.

In team meetings when things went awry, rather than a top-down, redirect-the-team-to-the-task-at-hand approach, Dave was able to get things back on track by asking how their ideas contributed to the bigger picture of the aspirations they had as a team. Some ideas were tabled for future considerations, and some new ideas emerged that were innovative to solving the problems at hand.

Not only was a new career path developed for Dave, the company grew because of his ability to connect the dots of aspirations of others with the work at hand, which resulted in innovative new solutions and retaining key, valuable employees.

The problem Dave untangled is that creating conversational space for stretch thinking takes a back seat to what we know, what went well, and what we need to work on. These conversations limit what is available. When we focus on what we do not know or what may not be apparent, ambitions and aspirations can emerge. When we understand who people want to become, we then can align personal ambitions with the business at hand. With conversations that stretch our thinking, we can begin to explore what may be possible.

While aspirations and expectations may seem like the same thing, they are not. They impact a very different part of the brain. Expectations and goals activate the neocortex. This part of the brain acts like a library of knowledge; it holds working memory and stored memory. It focuses on the past. Expectations can easily trigger a connotation of judgment and what *should* be done based on past experience, information, and results.

The effect of this triggered memory is that when the brain gets flooded with cortisol, people shut down and only see what is in front of them and what they already know or have experienced. This limits them to keep doing more of what they already are doing, thinking it will yield different results, which it usually does not.

When conversations expand beyond what we already know, including questions that we do not have the answers to, the prefrontal cortex or executive brain is triggered. The brain begins to open up and think in bigger, more expansive ways beyond the status quo. It allows others to dream big, create, innovate, and see what is possible. Many times we skip this step as a foundation for strategies, goals, and expectations. We fail to connect the dots of what we really want and how the work we are doing together can be the springboard to getting there.

One of my aspirations was to be involved in the lives of my grandchildren as they grew up. *Involved* to me meant more than just seeing them at Sunday dinners and special events. I wanted more than that. My daughter suggested perhaps I could pick them up from school and spend that time with them once a week. My response was, "Oh, that will not work." And out came the list of reasons why this could not be possible. I was in the past trap of the status quo.

In my head, I knew all of this, and if I continued to do what I already was doing, nothing would change. So, I asked myself a simple question: *What would it be like, what would it look like, to live my aspiration?* In spite of being able to control my schedule and create the space for this, there was fear and doubt that I could really commit to this.

Then the stretch thinking set in: *If you don't try you will never know what could be and what is possible. Decisions are not forever decisions; they can be tweaked and changed as the situation calls for it.* This pulled me forward to a trial run of after-school Wednesday dates. This trial has turned into the new standard of being involved.

The lesson I learned from that five-year-old preschool graduate was once I got clear on my aspiration and how I wanted to show up, the rest became a blueprint for action. It is so easy to get into action and figure out how to develop goals and expectations but miss the point of that bigger picture that pulls us forward.

As recounted in *The Art of Possibility* two salesmen in the early 1900s traveled from England to Africa to discover whether they could sell shoes there.[23] Independently, they sent telegrams back to England.

First salesman: *"Situation horrible. They don't wear shoes."*

Second salesman: *"Glorious opportunity. They don't have shoes yet."*

The first man saw nothing but the current situation as roadblocks and hurdles. The other saw nothing but opportunity. Leading conversations that focus on a world rich in possibility send a very clear message to your team, clients, and customers. Regardless of the current situation, there is the opportunity to look through a different lens to explore new paths, see the potential for greater success and fulfillment, and create meaningful change.

Conversational Shifters. There are practical actions we can take to shift into stretch conversations to focus on a world rich in possibility. Conversations that allow for this space encourage *what if . . . ?* thinking to emerge and shift conversational patterns from knowing to discovering what we have not thought of.

1. Shift from being a telling leader to an asking leader. This shifts the power from someone who has influence over others by virtue of position, authority, or expertise to someone who wants to create power with others. Instead of feeling like

you need to have all the answers to guide, direct, and decide everything, give permission to talk about aspirations. Ask questions that allow others to think out loud or be quiet as they contemplate. Listen to what they have to say.

2. Shift from saying only what you think others need to hear and sugarcoating the truth to speaking honestly and telling the truth with care and candor. Instead of judging, criticizing, or hiding the truth to protect people, set the tone of honesty. Honest talk is not mean talk; it is clear talk. You care enough to give feedback and talk about the situation to help others learn from past mistakes. Candor is telling the truth so you can find new and better ways for success together.

3. Shift from giving select information to certain people (protection) to having no sacred cows, and the involved people all hear the information (connection). It sets the stage to share information and exchange ideas within and between people and teams. This reduces the need to protect turf and breaks down barriers to test the waters and explore new territories. Allow differences of opinions and meld them into new ways of thinking; challenge the status quo through developing others' ideas and encouraging them to think differently together.

Conversational Breakers: *"We are doing well, so let's just keep going."* It accepts the status quo as the way things are and there is no space for freedom of new ideas, fresh perspectives, or building trust.

Conversational Makers: *"We are good at what we do, but what would it look like to be better?"* An openness to encourage stretch thinking builds trust. The results are innovation, higher levels of problem-solving to see different ways, and talking through unravelling challenges not yet thought about.

A common, underdeveloped conversational skill is asking questions for which you do not have the answer. You are an expert in your field; you have a vast array of experience, knowledge, education, and intelligence. It is easy to guide others to do what you want under the guise of shortening their learning curve or educating others. We are not taught how to talk about hopes, dreams, and ambitions. So, we settle for believing that it is easier to stick to the facts.

When we ask questions for which we do not have the answer, we bring out the potential in others, inspiring commitment and ownership of the future. It ignites new thinking, excitement, and empowerment. It engenders trust in a relationship that is made to last. It goes beyond open-ended questions in that these are content-specific, relevant inquiries to the topic being discussed that encourage others to paint a picture of what may be possible beyond the specific goal.

Here are a few examples of questions for which you do not have the answer to get you started:

- I'd like you to think big about you. What are your greatest aspirations, ambitions, or dreams for the future?
- What is the right thing for you to do to get to the next step?
- What do you think would happen if . . .?
- What would that look like?
- What does that mean to you?

- What does your timetable look like?
- What is important about that?
- If there were no limitations, what could we do?
- I want you to stretch yourself a bit on this project. What would help push you out of your comfort zone?
- I am not the expert in these things. What do you think?
- I value different opinions. What is your perspective?
- Here are our key challenges. What are your ideas on how to tackle them?
- It was a tough decision to make. What were the things you were thinking through? What was learned?

The more we can foster conversations that tap into the best in others, the more we create a world rich in opportunities for growth and learning. Stretch conversations are cocreated to encourage people to talk about their aspirations and consider options they had not considered. It supports them to embrace the future and what is possible, rather than fearing it and giving up on their dreams, setting small ambitions, or accepting the status quo. They are able to take risks and achieve new levels of success.

Stretch conversations align where we want to grow and how we can develop the supporting strategies, objectives, and goals to get us there. That is what makes a conversation that builds relationships, work groups, families, and cultures that last a lifetime.

MAKE IT OR BREAK IT

Principle #3: Stretch Thinking

1. Get clear on your own aspirations so you can easily lead others in this unique conversation.
2. Ask your clients/team what they aspire to, and what it means to them.
3. Connect the dots: Help them to see where they are and verbalize the possibilities with them.
4. Let your clients/team see your thought process using aspirations as the springboard for what is meaningful to them and what you can develop together.
5. No matter how big or small, all aspirations count. Don't assume you know theirs or that they are the same as yours.

CHAPTER 9

Principle #4: Discover Ideas

Every conversation is an opportunity to learn more about what really matters to someone. Human beings thrive on discovering more about each other, new avenues of thinking, new ideas, and being a contributing part of this. Discovery conversations make trusting relationships—a precursor for new ideas, innovation, creativity, loyalty, and engagement.

Many of our day-to-day conversations stay at the surface level and focus on the work at hand, the facts, and getting the job done. While this is important, if it's solely the focus of how we talk to others, the work gets done and people comply, but at the expense of them not feeling a sense of personal accomplishment, belonging, or that they matter. These conversations break relationships.

Sadly enough, many individuals, teams, and organizations operate from this state of distrust and fear. We go along to get along and fear that if we don't, someone else right behind us will. And when that happens, secret barriers and walls develop that separate us from each other. The bigger picture of what is going on remains hidden, selective facts are given, and people will not open up and talk about it. The best ideas and the best in people are locked up and never discovered.

The Science Of Discovering Ideas

The hippocampus is located in the center of the brain and is part of the limbic system. It has the big job of consolidating information from short-term memory to long-term memory. It is very mathematical, predictable, and maps *every interaction* we have had with another human being.

If I have a positive interaction with you, it gets mapped. The next time I meet you, I look forward to talking with you. There is a level of openness in connecting with you.

If I have a less than positive interaction with you, it gets mapped. Even the thought of having a conversation with you automatically makes me feel cautious and protective because I remember the conversation we had. There may be fear of being judged, looking weak, being wrong, being excluded, or not knowing where I stand, or worry over what I can and can't say. This absence of connection moves people into protection, skepticism, and distrust.

If there are mixed reviews on interactions—some interactions went well and some did not—I feel uncertain of whether to trust or not. Trust and distrust live in different parts of the brain; they can coexist. Lower trust means higher uncertainty, and the higher the trust we feel, the less uncertainty we feel. Uncertainty results in playing it safe, going along to get along.

We cannot change how the brain works. Conversations that activate fear are driven by cortisol. People are afraid to share and afraid to trust, and in this fear, we try to prove our point and that we are right. Conversations that activate trust are driven by oxytocin, which makes it easier to share, as there is a feeling of safety and inclusion—that we won't be rejected or made fun of. It is a game changer!

Mary and David are colleagues and have been friends for a long time. Over lunch, they catch up about what they are doing at work. David excitedly describes an idea he has come up. Mary looks at David with a smile and jokingly responds with, "This is another 'good idea' just like all the others before. When are you going to stick with what you are doing and really get good at that instead of having your head in the clouds?"

Can you imagine how David feels? Mary was considered a friend and a confidant David could share ideas with, but now he feels blindsided, discounted, and hurt. Even though the comment was made jokingly, he secretly wonders if she really cares enough to hear him out, worries where he stands with her, and what he should share.

Mary instantly notices his startled expression and that he physically pulled back from her. She knows immediately that what she meant to say did not land. She apologizes for her hurtful sarcasm and says, "What I really wanted to say instead was, 'How does this fit in with what you are already doing?'"

Did this break their relationship? No, but it certainly was a comment David remembered for a long time that caused him to be careful and hesitant about what he would share with Mary in the future. I learned this because David is my friend and long after our conversation, he was able to tell me this. (Yes, Mary was me.)

What I learned is that we are all human and no matter how good our intentions are, we say things in the moment that miss the mark. People withhold their ideas, thoughts, opinions, and feelings. Leading quality conversations by the words you use and the things you say triggers chemical reactions in the brain—toward connection and discovery or protection and withholding—that make or break the conversation.

Shifts to discovery conversations are organized around the concepts of the PRIME model. To get ahead of the curve to minimize fear and uncertainty in conversations, we can lead and respond in the moment, encouraging discovery rather than withdrawing into secrecy. Others need to feel you listen and care enough to discover who they are and what really matters to them. It's only then that they feel free and safe to share what is really in their hearts and minds, making a quality conversation that builds lifelong relationships.

1. **P**ersonal Connection
2. **R**adical Transparency
3. **I**ntention–Impact Gap
4. **M**eaning For Me
5. **E**mpathy

1. Personal Connection

First impressions matter. Before any words are spoken, your brain has taken a reading on the people in front of you, whether they are friends and it is safe to connect, or are foes and you move into protection. It happens in less than a tenth of a second. The problem is this first impression leaves a lasting impression, but it may not be right. That's why it is important to have the very first words out of your mouth be words that signal openness to create an emotional connection. This triggers the executive brain and calms anxieties and fears others may have.

So stop wasting the space with small talk about the latest weather, traffic, or sports scores. Get right to the heart of the matter. Offer a warm handshake (or perhaps an elbow bump) and a kind smile, and look into their eyes to let them know you are happy to share time with them. Tell them in your own words. It opens your heart to focus on them and it opens their heart to feel they are the most important person at that moment.

Here is the caveat: You must care enough to be interested in others. If you see clients as your paycheck or your staff as assets to be managed or costs to be controlled, you have missed the point. If you say it and don't mean it, they will know it.

Conversational Intimacy

Conversations build bridges to personal connections. It all starts with asking questions and learning about others in a nonintrusive way. Discovery questions, specifically questions for which you do not have the answers, encourage you to learn about them and they can share at their own time and pace.

Imagine personal relationships are a set of three concentric circles.

- In the very outside circle are things everyone knows, basic facts and data—how the world sees me.
- The middle circle contains things that can be shared easily, like experiences, interests, likes and dislikes, family—how I operate in the world.

- The innermost circle is who I really am and what I really think and feel—who I am and what matters to me. It is my personal identity: what I am really good at, what I want to get better at, what I learned from the times I've failed, ideas I have, and how I see myself. This is largely my private world. You earn the right to enter into this innermost circle once you have demonstrated by your conversation that you listen and care about me.

Business is personal. When we take a few minutes to get personal with people, discover who they are and what matters to them, we open the parts of the brain designed for connection. Connecting with others at a human level results in conversations that build a strong foundation for healthy relationships; sharing and discovering together lead to innovation, problem-solving, inclusion, and the next level of trust.

As a new executive director for a team of fifty people, organized into eight different divisions, with a matrix relationship with twenty different departments of over 200 people, I wondered how I could ever personally connect with all these people.

Using the circle model of conversational intimacy, I started with my direct team. We had introductory conversations where my goal was to learn more about them and their work and how they interacted with the organization we worked for. Informally, we talked about facts like where they grew up and went to school, what working life was like for them, their family, what their hobbies were, what was going on for them right then, and one piece of advice they would give me to be better in my role. And when they asked the same questions of me, which some did and others did not, I answered with the same honesty they had extended to me.

It was brief and clear; I let them take the time they needed to talk about themselves personally. For some, it led to a deeper, more connected conversation. Others chose to share only a few words in response, and that was okay. The seeds for remembering something personal, noting there was a person besides the business at hand, were planted.

With some of the other 200 people who were my collaboration partners, I had individual conversations over time. With everyone, I listened and made notes of what they shared. Before delving into the immediate business topic at hand, I opened the conversation with something that was important to them. "I remember at the last meeting, you mentioned you had a wedding/research paper/grant/presentation/trip coming up. How did that go for you?"

Business is personal and there is nothing as important as taking the time to be interested and getting to know the people you work with.

2. Radical Transparency

Be yourself, everyone else is already taken.

—Oscar Wilde

Transparency has become a hot topic. You can hardly pick up a book or read an article without tips, systems, and scripts on *how* to be transparent. While there is no question that transparency results in astounding engagement, productivity, profitability, retention, alignment, and whatever else frays our ability to connect and trust with each other, you must first know what happens in the brain so you can know how to create the conversational space for transparency.

In any conversation, there is an interesting paradox of uncertainty that occurs in the brain, whether you are aware of it or not. On one hand, the brain craves certainty, predictability, and to know what will happen. But, on the other hand, conversations have a life of their own. Rarely is it humanly possible to predict the outcome of a conversation with a high degree of certainty.

This uncertainty creates fear. From this fear, the unspoken inner dialogue begins running in the back of your mind as *I wonder if . . .? How will this . . .? What will really happen?* So we wait, go silent, or even shut down and don't speak because we feel unsure and fearful.

With fear running the show, you may be unknowingly sabotaging your ability to be transparent to build trust and loyalty. You tell people what you think they need to know when you think they need to know it. You protect people from the real truth because you don't know how they will respond. You protect yourself from what you don't know and don't ask for help. Patrick Lencioni describes this as the root cause of distrust.[24] We cannot be open, transparent, and vulnerable to ask for help and support each other.

I call this the *illusion* of transparency. We have all experienced this. We enter into conversations thinking we know the agenda, only to be blindsided by an unspoken, hidden agenda.

- A performance review for a stellar employee starts out with, "Job well done! But what we really need to talk about is that your position is being eliminated."

- Financial planning that leads to, "The best option is buying this service or product to protect your future."
- A leader asks for ideas from the team but in the next statement says, "This is what we are going to do."
- A first-time meeting with someone who says they want to learn about you but all they talk about is themselves.

No one is exempt from conversational experiences veiled in the *illusion* of transparency. These conversations are stored away in our brain's memory bank. The next time a conversation even comes close being similar to this, we shut down and tune out. We don't care to hear what the other is saying; we retreat into our own thinking. We fail to engage, connect, and be open to discover.

Your level of transparency directly impacts what others feel free to share. So *how* do you create the space for transparency in conversations?

You model radical transparency and give permission for others to do the same. You encourage more open conversations where people challenge one another in search of a solution rather than proving themselves right.

In his book, *Principles,* Richard Dalio describes radical transparency as the ability to know how to take things ordinary people would hide, put them on the table—particularly mistakes, problems, and weaknesses—and look at them together.[25]

Radical Transparency Is Straight, Honest Talk. Radically transparent talk is not always easy talk. It requires you to share what you can, what you know, and what you don't know, and understand the difference.

It is less important for me to be right than to get it right. While we may think we are being helpful and justified in telling others how to do things and fall into shorten-their-learning-curve thinking, we eliminate the challenge of searching for the right solution. This implies your way is the only way; there are no other options.

Be courageous enough to say what we really think and establish that we can agree to disagree. If these conversational ground rules are not addressed, the win-lose mentality takes over and we fight to win at any cost. This mentality leaves us feeling uncertain, fearful, and wanting to protect ourselves; we will not be transparent or honest to openly talk about what we really think.

Radical Transparency Is Not Total Transparency. In sharing information that is not yours to share, boundaries of confidentiality must be held. You may know personal health issues or circumstances of people who have confided in you. Or, perhaps you know of internal conversations that relate to security and business operations. That is not yours to share.

To discern what is and what is not yours to share, it is important to ask yourself the following questions. *Why am I withholding information? Am I hiding something that needs to be said? Is it important and meaningful? Does it add value? Is it mine to share?*

To discern what to share, it is helpful to answer two questions first. *Why am I sharing this? How will it serve the conversation?* If you are sharing just to get it off your chest and feel better, it distracts from the conversation and does not serve the person you are in front of. Sharing to allow others to see what you may be struggling with or need support in serves the relationship, as it opens the door to deeper understanding.

Radical Transparency Is Not Mean Talk. Let me be clear. It does not give you the right or authority to blame, accuse, or in any way, shape, or form belittle others to make yourself feel big. It is not unheard of that politics, personality, and positional power can lead to backstabbing, water cooler conversations, and a feeling of self-righteousness with a better-than-thou attitude. That is the antithesis of transparency. That is not right; it is mean, self-serving talk.

Radical Transparency Requires A Conversational Roadmap That Is Cocreated. A conversational roadmap includes both context and content. *Context* answers the question of *why* we are meeting. Clarity of purpose such as information, discussion, or decision avoids misunderstanding. *Content* addresses *what* you will talk about. An *agenda* creates such a roadmap. When the agenda is open to other ideas of what should be addressed and it is not just what you think is important, it empowers others and sends a message that, "we are in this together; we are working together."

At times, we need to hold the conversational roadmap (or agenda) loosely, be open to influence, and be flexible enough to allow the other person to say what needs to be said, to clear the air. You have cocreated the context and content, and then out of the blue, the other person blurts out that it is hard for them to focus because they just got news that has turned their world upside down. Instead of stepping over it or giving some flat response such as, "I understand. Let's refocus on what we were discussing," offer the opportunity to talk through it, if they wish.

Unanticipated twists and turns in conversations give permission for others to be human and share what is important to them.

Radical Transparency Never Judges. There are no right or wrong questions or thoughts, just different viewpoints. Don't judge. Instead, take the standpoint of valuing differing opinions as a way of learning a broader perspective. A different view just may be the fuel to think about challenges in a new way. "I never thought about it that way before; tell me more."

Sometimes we feel embarrassed or foolish asking questions we think we should know the answer to. It requires a willingness to explore differing ideas and further steps that can be taken. Something as simple as, "I didn't quite get that and I really want to understand. Could you explain that again?"

Listen first to what others are trying to say and ask them directly for their opinions. Don't guess about what you think they said. Wait to hear their explanation before you talk, then do so openly and share your knowledge freely. Frame how you express your opinions as opinions, not mandates. "This is my opinion on the matter, but I am open to learn other ways it might fit in with what we are talking about."

Transparency shows up consistently in your conversations and signals you are honest, open, and have no secret agenda. People like to know things; it gives them a sense of comfort and confidence if they know nothing is hidden—no hidden agendas, meanings, secrets, or failure to disclose. When you discover what matters to other and their ideas, you support and help them to give words to what is unknown and lurking just beneath the surface.

Radical Transparency And Vulnerability. Without transparency and vulnerability, trust cannot develop. The quality of conversations you lead builds transparency. I can be factual and transparent with what is going on and tell you what is on my mind. I can describe a situation that is real and honest, and not hide the facts.

However, when I attach an emotion to the situation that is on my mind, it transforms into vulnerability. Vulnerability defined by the expert Brene Brown is "not winning or losing; it's having the courage to show up and be seen when we have no control over the outcome."[26]

The moment I let you into my world of what my situation is and how it feels and impacts me, transparency becomes vulnerability. It is taking action in such a way that you can see and verify what I am saying. You no longer hide and fear I will judge you, but know I listen and care. You feel emotionally connected to me. These conversations make a relationship that lasts.

Doing The Right Thing. One of my CEO clients was transparent with how he learned about the guiding value of doing the right thing:

"I learned from my mother the importance of doing the right thing as a child after spending a few days in 'Mother's jail' to think about why I stole candy from the store. It forever left the value in me that I must do the right thing, no matter what, even when no one else notices."

However, a transformation occurred in his conversations when he took transparency to vulnerability. Adding in the emotions of the situation, the impact it created for him, and the lesson he learned that he was willing to share with others, the story became this one:

"I learned from my mother the importance of doing the right thing as a child after spending a few days 'Mother's jail' to think about why I stole candy from the store. I remember feeling punished for something that was wrong, even to this day. I feel embarrassed talking about it, wondering what you will think of me as a child thief. More importantly, as I spent time thinking about it with Mom's guidance, I realized the real lesson: I had gifts and talents to make my own way. I did not have to steal. I could get a job, earn money, and in doing so, earn money to be of service to others. Although the days of collecting pop bottles, mowing grass, and shining shoes are over, the lesson sticks with me and is a foundational belief and core principle of how I run this company. Do the right thing, all the time, to the best of your ability, and especially when others are not watching."

He shares this with his team, taking the lead to show transparency and vulnerability as a role model for them. He recently opened a client appreciation event with this story. The response from his high net worth clients? An awkward silence, then, nervous laughter turned into applause . . . with a few clients from the audience shouting, "That's the guy we know!"

When emotions are added to a situation and vulnerability is created, the real you is out in the open. It impacts how others feel. Authentically being yourself, putting words and emotions to the situation and verbalizing it to others, deepens their trust and understanding of you. You have gained the trusted advisor status that no marketing message or materials can buy.

When leaders are vulnerable, are more open to discovery and sharing with others, they signal that they are emotionally available. This triggers the prefrontal cortex to flood the brain with oxytocin, creating connection and bonding through shared experiences, improving the performance of everyone. Vulnerable leaders inspire through authenticity and humanity. Tough leaders inspire through fear and intimidation. Which will you become?

3. Intention–Impact Gap

The purpose of discovery conversations is to connect and understand what is going on with others that will enable us to move forward in a positive direction.

When your conversations go awry, one of the most common causes is that an intention–impact gap has occurred. *Intention* is what you want to happen. *Impact* is the receiver's experience of what happened. This occurs when what you had in your head and the thought you conveyed was not what was heard. Your words or actions are not understood or are misinterpreted by the other person.

We all make assumptions. Assumptions represent how we see the world based on our unique personal experiences and circumstances. I bring my assumptions into conversations (by thinking that what I am saying is understood by you). You bring your assumptions to conversations that may not be the same way I see things. Instead of talking over each other, discovery conversations open up the discussion in real time so we can understand each other and the assumptions we may be making. Discovery conversations support us in decoding and aligning intentions, and developing a positive impact that results in broader insights to work together.

Underneath every conversation is an intention, whether you are aware of it or not. Self-awareness guides your intentions, intentions influence your conversations, and conversations influence your results. Use self-awareness before conversations to be clear about why are you having this discussion. When you are clear, you can share that with others.

Consider this scenario. Heidi is the director of operations and Chris reports to her. They are evaluating the client experience process and decide the best way to start is to examine the current process.

The following week, they meet to share what they have learned. Chris excitedly pulls out the flow diagram of how the whole process can be changed. He intends to have a positive impact on the company by designing a new system, using his creative perspective to make things better.

Immediately, Heidi pulls back; the intention of the evaluation was to examine the current practice and discover where the bottlenecks are, not to create a whole new process. She has in her mind (and in her intention) a logical step-by-step analysis to first understand the problem, and then to take the systematic steps to change the process. She feels a little ruffled and interprets the work as beyond what was asked for, and besides, this is not really his job. She reminds Chris, "We need to go back to the drawing board and figure out what is not working before we implement a new process."

The impact of this conversation? Chris feels dismissed and wonders why his boss even asked to discuss this in the first place if she was not willing to discover and talk through new ideas. Heidi feels like she really blew it. She was surprised at the extent of the work Chris did even though it was not how she thought it should have been done, but not being able to express this, she shut down Chris.

Heidi is a client of mine, so we were able to debrief the conversation by understanding the intention–impact gap. I share this case example and debrief process with you so you can learn and apply the intention–impact gap to your conversations that just might be missing the mark.

- Clarify the intentions of the conversation, not the content of the work to be done—that is secondary. Instead of removing emotion, we include it to figure out how to manage our own emotions better as they come up in conversations.

- Why was Heidi having this conversation?

- As a result of this conversation, how did she want Chris—the person—to feel? Heidi wanted to tap into the expertise and knowledge Chris had to come up with the best options and work in partnership with him.

- Using the past as a learning tool for the future, I asked Heidi about the impact of what she said. Heidi remembered Chris physically moved back in his chair, rolled his eyes, and responded, "Okay, what do you want?" This is exactly when I knew what she had said was all wrong and moved him into protection.

- I asked Heidi, "What was going on in your head—what were you saying or thinking to yourself that

> prompted your response?" It's not enough to be self-aware; we must use this to shape conversations. Heidi was surprised at the in-depth consideration Chris has given to his work and did not know what to say or do. For a moment, she honestly thought Chris wanted to be the rising star and "I had better get him on the right track. I am the boss, and this is how we do things." Instead of responding with discovery questions such as how he had gotten to this point or what he was thinking, her automatic reaction was "That is not what I asked for."

While we cannot take back the words that are spoken, we are all human and sometimes say things in conversation we did not mean or were misinterpreted. We can start another conversation, a do-over.

This is what a do-over can look like: Start with an invitation to another conversation with clarity of intention and impact.

"Chris, I would like to have another conversation about your ideas. I think I jumped the gun and dismissed them before fully understanding all that went into it."

Discovery questions: Instead of judgment, encourage sharing.

"Talk me through what you were thinking." Listen. Stop talking. Wonder what is possible.

Instead of what we cannot do, what *can* we do? The reality may be there are resource constraints and other work priorities that make a complete overhaul too much right now. What steps or pieces can you use to start making incremental changes? Small hinges can swing open big doors.

Let's build this together. Now that you have cleared the air, it is time for the specifics of the plan.

"Given all the other priorities we are working on right now, what do you think should be the top two priorities for this quarter? In subsequent quarters and timeframes, we can build on these fundamentals."

No one is perfect at conversations all the time. We are human. The lesson I have learned and teach my clients about being human is that once we get really clear on our intentions and how the words we use impact what others hear, feel, and think, we can use a conversational do-over to check ourselves with the intention–impact thinking. We can lead future conversations to bring out understanding and the best in people and their ideas by ideas by tapping into the brain that is designed for connection.

4. Meaning For Me

Set up conditions that are not about you. A "me orientation" is anything that keeps us focused on ourselves rather than the people we are in conversation with. Any form of this preoccupation with our own agenda is focusing on something other than the client.

Let's be honest here. There is nothing we think more about than ourselves. It is our favorite pastime. The next time you are not engaged in a task and are just being, notice what you are thinking about. Chances are, it is about you. What you said, what you've got to do next, what you are planning to do, what you didn't do, and on and on. Sure, it may involve other people, but it is in relation to you!

Many of you have been trained and rewarded to be a problem-solver, not a problem-listener. You feel safe focusing on technical mastery and how that solves the problem and believe that is sufficient to engage others in conversations. Driven, ambitious, technically excellent people focus on their own performance and how they are winning at the work they do. They look for confirmation of their competitive development and that what they are doing is right. Winning or losing conversations break a relationship every time.

Here is why: Our brains process faster than the words we hear; we drop out of conversations after twelve to eighteen seconds to make sense of what we think was said. We disconnect from the actual conversation going on and stop listening to what the other person is saying. Your own thoughts about what is important and what you can do to solve this take over. You know you can get to the bottom of this. This premature problem-solving is based on surface information, analysis, and content from your perspective, giving you the competitive advantage.

It takes over before you know what is really important to the person speaking. To compound the situation, you start thinking about how you will respond. You wonder what you will say to keep the upper hand. This triggers fears that range from embarrassment or ignorance—*maybe I cannot solve the problem*—to loss of your own security and reputation—*maybe I am not as smart as I think I am or as others have told me I am.* To cover this uncomfortable situation, you resort back to your old thinking and conversational patterns of winning others over by showing them what you know. So you talk more to fill the void of this uncomfortable feeling. And the more you talk, the better you feel, so the more you talk. Your brain gets a hit of the reward chemical dopamine, and you keep talking about what you think is important and how you can solve this once and for all.

The impact of this conversational pattern is that the other person feels forgotten. No trust has developed. The client or employee is interested in having their own challenge or problem understood and getting to the real meaning of what they were trying to say. They want to hear and feel that you understand them. There are many complexities, people, positions, politics, and emotions that are underneath the surface that influence the situation. They want to know that you care enough to really discover what these nuances are and when you do, you will earn the right to help them. It is only then that they will open up and share with you what is really going on.

When you learn how to recognize and manage the "me orientation," you can lead healthy, productive conversations—conversations that connect with others, get to the bottom of what really matters to others, and remain focused on them. Others will want to work with you, take your advice, and stay with you.

To move conversations from *me* to *we*, start with calming your own fear and anxiety of moving from a problem-solver to a problem-listener. It is your willingness to reframe your own mindset and attitude. Remember, conversations are not a sprint to win, but rather a marathon of commitment and mutually understanding what needs to be resolved.

The most important gift you can give another is to listen to discover and help them verbalize the issues at hand and what that means for them. Don't just ask open-ended questions, but thought-provoking, truth-telling questions that give permission for others to tell the story of how they go to where they are today. Ask questions you do not have the answer to, such as their aspirations, what the future looks like to them, and what really is behind the issue. Don't be afraid to respectfully acknowledge their emotions. And, if the time is right, share with them your experience and the relevancy of what you learned from a similar situation and how that applies to what you are talking about.

Be critically self-aware about how much of the conversational space you spend talking. It is easy to disguise talking as educating, informing, and glorifying the benefits you offer. When you recognize you have monopolized the conversation, you can turn it around by saying something like, "I get so excited and passionate when talking about the work I do, that I have been doing all the talking. I apologize. Enough about me. I want to learn about you."

You can only add real value *after* listening rather than trying to do that *during* listening. It is the give-and-take dialogue with others that makes a quality conversation grow into a healthy relationship. When they know you are interested and care enough to deeply listen to them, then, and only then, will they feel safe enough to open up and share what is really on their mind instead of withholding the real truth of their situation.

This sounds easier than it is. Learning to focus on the other person is a lifelong learning experience. Be willing to discover, engage, and openly explore the true issues, to be of service before selling, to give away your expertise in pursuit of a better problem definition.

Others make up their minds about you very quickly. First impressions matter. If it is all about you, it will not be a good impression. The reward for having the best-defined problem through discovering what really matters to others is that there is a level and feeling of trust that develops. Not only will you listen to learn, but you have the courage to say the hard things in service of them.

5. Empathy

"Nobody cares how much you know until they know how much you care."

—Theodore Roosevelt

Empathy is the willingness to step into the shoes of another person, to see the situation through their eyes and their perspective, and to understand their needs and emotions. It is stepping into the conversational circle to discover—not judge—how they see things to understand what their world is like and the experiences they've had that influenced them.

If you have had a similar situation to the one you hear, your long-term memory bank is activated and you actually may feel what another is feeling. If you have not had similar experiences, you may not really understand their situation. Emotions, however, are universal. Empathy is about matching emotions, not necessarily the situation. To empathetically connect with others, we identify how someone feels and use that as the base for understanding.

When we seek to understand the needs and emotions of another and see the world through their eyes, we are better able to identify what they are feeling and what it is like to be in their situation. The mirror neurons located below the prefrontal cortex are activated and create empathetic feelings. Empathy fuels connection and a resonance between people, and builds a bridge of understanding that strengthens trust.

Four qualities of empathy outlined by Brene Brown are:

1. Being able to see the world as others see it. This requires putting our stuff aside to see the situation through another's eyes.

2. Being nonjudgmental. Judgment of another person's situation discounts their experience and is an attempt to protect ourselves from the pain of the situation.

3. Understanding another person's feelings. We need to be in touch with our personal feelings to understand someone else's. This also requires putting aside "us" to focus on the other.

4. Communicating our understanding of that person's feelings. Rather than saying, "At least . . ." or, "It could be worse . . ." try, "I've been there, and I know what that is like," or a statement as simple as, "It sounds like you are in a hard place now. Tell me more about it."[27]

Business Empathy. Empathy has been called the new leadership competency, and here's why: Being able to empathize with others, to understand and connect with their emotions is critical; without it, it is tough to read the emotional climate of an organization, which affects everything from employee productivity and culture-building retention to client work. Feeling heard and understood is a human need. It is also how we connect, help, and support one another.

Empathy is important, but why is it so hard? There are many misinterpretations and fears around empathy:

- **Talking about emotions is soft and a sign of weakness.** Being empathetic triggers the fear of showing emotions. With this fear, the power to connect turns off and we become less sensitive to others' perspectives.
- **Empathy means agreeing with others.** Understanding a different perspective does not mean you agree—it means you are open to acknowledge and understand what they think and how they feel. You care enough about someone personally to actively and respectfully challenge them in the decisions they make instead of staying silent for fear of damaging the relationship and operating from the idea that "the client knows best."
- **Empathy means you are obligated to do what they want.** You are not responsible for another's emotions. You are not responsible for making others feel better, and it is highly unlikely that your response will. What will make it better is that you connected and created a safe space for them to feel their own emotions and understand their experience.

Empathy In Action. Empathy is a good starting point, but it is not enough. You can get so caught up in the feelings of others that you are not very helpful. When you understand this emotional contagion is counterproductive, you transform empathy into compassion by asking yourself how you can support this person. The prefrontal cortex is activated and opens up opportunities for problem-solving rather than just the experience. Compassion is not feeling *with* someone, it is feeling *for* someone. They are not alone since you care enough to support them to work through their uncomfortable situation, but you are not attached to the outcome of what action they will take.

MAKE IT OR BREAK IT

Principle #4: Discover Ideas

1. Get to know others and let them know you on a personal level to create a foundation of trust.
2. Be first to role model your own vulnerability before you ask others to share.
3. Align your intention, what you want to happen, with your impact, which is the experience of how the other is receiving your message. Ask questions that go deeper, such as, "What impact would this have on you?"
4. Your value comes from being of service to others with a joint process of discovery to define what matters to them.
5. Move beyond the facts and the numbers to a curiosity of what it might be like to be them and live in their world.
6. Move into empathy in action with compassion—kindness through objectivity to support and be of benefit to others.

CHAPTER 10

Principle #5: Explore Meaning

In my mother's bedroom, in the top right-hand drawer, was a brown leather box that she warned me to never touch. Being five years old and still having the wonderful gift of curiosity, I carefully removed the forbidden box, opened it, and saw in it the beautiful necklace of white beads—pearls—that she wore on special occasions. My curiosity kept growing and I wondered how I could put on the necklace, just like my mom did. I tried to open the clasp but it wouldn't budge. *There has got to be a way*, so I pulled and tugged with mighty determination until the strand gave way to my efforts and I was surrounded by a sea of pearls rolling all over the floor.

In enters my mom. You know that feeling you get as a parent when your kids are too quiet, they must be up to something, most likely trouble? I was in deep trouble. She gave me a stern lecture. There was something about curiosity killing the cat that I didn't quite get. What I did get was something about being a troublemaker, why couldn't I do what she asked, and spending an hour in my room to think about it.

I learned I should do what my mom tells me to do. I chuckle at that experience now, and am amazed how we use that old saying, "curiosity killed the cat," to shut down what we think is unnecessary investigation, experimentation, and learning.

Curiosity is an innate human quality. As children, we want to understand how the world around us operates to make sense of all we do not know. As we grow and develop, curiosity does not go away but transforms into acquiring knowledge, information, and understanding.

When we open up conversations that encourage exploring, the prefrontal cortex is activated and we begin to think about things in new ways. We can tap into the capacity we all have to imagine, create, discover, and invent. Humans thrive on exploring ideas; it creates energy and excitement.

Francesca Gino makes the business case for curiosity. Her research identifies that curiosity in business results in fewer decision-making errors, more innovation, positive changes in creative and noncreative jobs, reduced group conflict, and better communication and team performance.[28]

The conversations we lead may be undermining exploring as a conversational principle. It is easy to focus on getting things done and results. Too many ideas lead to options that could result in a costly mess. Or questioning the status quo does not produce useful information, even though it may lead to not settling for the first possible solution and can yield better remedies. We get in a rut of proclaiming and telling people what to do—essentially thinking for them.

Leading curious conversation is unchartered territory for many. It implies you do not have the answer. This is implicit both for the lead and the client/team. This triggers the fear response—fear that we will be judged as incompetent or not as smart as we expected ourselves to be, that we should have all the answers, and know what to do, but we might not. We expect knowing and get trapped in conversations focused on what we know rather than being willing to explore other ideas and fresh perspectives.

We all have had experiences where we tried to talk about a different way of doing things or thought out loud, only to get the response, "Stick to what you know, that will never work," or "This is a disaster waiting to happen." We probably said to ourselves, *I will never do that again.* Our memory is wired to stay in protection mode. We move away from conversations that explore options to conversations that are "safer."

Go back to brain science. Every interaction is mapped in the hippocampus, the memory part of our brain. Many of us have been rewarded for knowing the right answer to the teacher's questions, the right solution to the company's problems. What we know is based on past experiences and education is safe and secure. Our brain recognizes this pattern. We get stuck in *knowing.*

Imagine you had a boss who belittled your performance, blamed you for a project that went off track, or even jokingly said, "That's just stupid." How willing would you be to explore different ideas? Instead of risking being made fun of, feeling like we don't fit in, being embarrassed in front of others, and not wanting to be called disagreeable, we clam up and go along to get along.

Imagine you are working with a client who seems to be dragging their feet in getting you information to move their plan forward. You respond with an explanation of what you need. You may ask them why they did not get it to you and even offer to help them. How willing do you think the client will be to tell you what is really on their mind about the missing paperwork?

Imagine you were talking to your partner about a great charter school you just heard about and say you want to visit, but your partner responds, "What we are doing works; that's how I was educated and I turned out fine. There is no need for this." What is the likelihood of exploring this idea further?

Whether it is work, client relationships, or talking with your partner, many conversations close the down the door to exploring and move the other person into protection or uncertainty.

This results in:

- Little or no engagement with others in the decision-making process
- Lack of cooperative relationships
- Communication that focuses on the status quo
- Missed opportunities to explore new ideas, new ways of thinking, innovation, and solving problems with a different approach

To lead conversations that explore instead of knowing, we need to learn how to create the right environment to open up the prefrontal cortex to activate trust, rather than being hostage to the past and the amygdala that activates distrust.

"Nine out of 10 people disagree with my idea, which sends a very clear message — nine out of 10 people are idiots!"

Put Curiosity Back In Conversations

According to the work done by John Medina in his book, *Brain Rules*, the human brain can only think of one idea at a time. When a question is posed, it overtakes the thought process to answer that question. It cannot contemplate anything else.[29]

Applying this to exploring conversations, many times we close down curiosity and focus on knowing, judging, or even criticizing new ideas. Asking a curious question such as, "How do you see this?" subtly opens up conversations and just thinking about doing something can shift your perception and later, body chemistry. It hijacks the brain in a powerful way. The moment you hear a question, you literally cannot think of anything else.

Curiosity squelches judgment in the brain with questions. Exploring questions resets the conversation and your brain focuses on finding the answer to what it does not know, rather than focusing on what it does know.

Integrating the principles we have discussed to set up healthy conversations, curiosity can be infused when you have the intention and the skill.

1. **Set the context, purpose, and intention of your conversation.** This means setting the purpose of the meeting, the logistics, and what will be talked about. When this is done, anxiety is reduced and the brain is triggered to think this is safe. It is critical to verbalize that this conversation is a time and place to open up and talk about things we have been thinking about and wanting to say but have not really had the chance to talk about.

2. **Prepare to shift to curiosity.** No doubt about it, a curious mindset may be counterintuitive to what you have been taught, what you know, and what you have done. You were born innately curious, and now it's time to tap into that curiosity. Expect the unexpected, prepare for things transpiring, and trust whatever is going to happen will be good with a favorable outcome. Assume the best; look with an open heart.

   When you shift your thinking, you shift your conversations:

   - From knowing all the answers to there is more that I can learn
   - From thinking the status quo is good to wondering what can make us better
   - From feeling others will judge you to feeling others value looking for answers together

3. **Operate from the right level of conversation.**

   Level One: Your conversation is in a question-and-answer format; it confirms what you know, but you don't engage the other person and what they are thinking or feeling. There is no emotional connection or trust.

   Level Two: You are set in your point of view and focus on how can you can influence this person to agree with you. You ask leading questions. This results in conditional trust and connection.

   Level Three: You are willing to explore a different opinion and are open and willing to discover what you do not know. This opens the brain to trust.

4. **Cocreate the guidelines of conversation.** Clarify how you will talk to each other and how you will hold each other to this standard. Make a curiosity pact. For example: *Comments will support us in learning better together, so there will be no judgments about questions that haven't been asked before; instead, we will get curious to ask more and understand more.*

5. **Use specific skills for an exploring conversation.** On a whim, a dare, and a good deal, I bought a class on improvisation for a charity's silent auction. Secretly, I thought, *Maybe there is a new career awaiting me as stand-up comedian*. Then, reality hit. *Probably not, but nothing ventured, nothing gained.*

   What I did learn was nothing short of amazing as it applies to conversations, staying in the moment, and responding to others from a place of not knowing. Asking a different question or giving a different kind of comment leads to a very different conversation—one that evokes a sense of curiosity and cocreates a mutually beneficial conversation that opens the doors to a deeper and more meaningful connection.

Accept what was said and build on it. It is not about agreeing or accepting everything said, nor is it about dismissing others or not asking why. It is about keeping the conversation moving through curious *how* or *what* questions:

How did that happen? What happened next?

How did it impact you or the situation?

How did that make you feel and influence you? What did you do?

What did we learn?

What could we consider?

How can we use this to find a new, different, or positive result?

A mix of questions and responses contributes to the conversation. If the conversation is primarily questions, if feels unnatural and like an interrogation. Sprinkle in commonalities of experiences and your point of view:

Thank you for sharing; I had an experience similar to that.

I was thinking something along those lines.

I have another way to look at this.

If we could do things differently, what would that look like?

There are no mistakes, just opportunities; no criticism or judgment or bad ideas. Using a "Yes, and . . .?" question continues the conversation, encourages sharing, and can create a call to action.

And, what happened next?

And, how can we build on this?

And, what's on the other side we have not talked about or considered?

When Conversations Get Stuck, We're Stuck!

Patterns are useful since they are is the brain's way of organizing so much coming to us all the time. In contrast, the brain does not see trying to generate new ideas or new ways of looking at situations as very helpful. It takes effort, therefore, to access new thought patterns, create a different perspective, or imagine a solution that was not there before.

Conversations are a back-and-forth dialogue. At any point in this dialogue, a range of decisions are made: *How much will I share? How honest and forthcoming will I be? If I answer truthfully, will this put me at a disadvantage?* This uncertainty often leads us to protection mode and we get stuck into an old pattern of thinking.

Opening up curious conversations for exploration can feel risky because we don't do it often and we've had patterns of conversations and experiences that were unproductive. Those are stored in the hippocampus and signal danger, *Don't go there! Remember what happened last time you did!*

Even with the best of intentions, our attempts to be curious in conversations may fall flat or get no response. So, when we ask people to explore different ways of thinking, to open up new avenues and find what is unknown, the response may be nothing short of that deer-in-the-headlights look. Is it any wonder that when we ask for new ideas, people cannot seem to come up with anything?

To interrupt this stuck pattern and bring in a fresh perspective, nudge the conversation to one of exploring by using the skills of R3: reframe, refocus, and redirect. These are powerful ways to regulate your own chemistry so you can lead conversations to elevate the communication of everyone involved; it gives you the ability to move into different conversations and enable others to explore, share wisdom, and allow new insights and ideas to emerge.

Reframe: It is so much more than being able to find the silver lining in any situation. A reframing "flips the switch" to reset the conversation and open other ways to interpret the situation—moving from negative to positive to enable exploring.

Refocus: Take the context of the current situation and put it into a bigger picture. Move the perspective from what we know to what we can discover.

Redirect: Open up the conversational space to explore what else may be possible and other actions that could be taken. You want to "nudge" people into a different direction without creating fear and resistance.

Take that boss who thought your idea was stupid.

> Boss: *The project went off track by a week. What was going on with your team?* (Understand the situation)
>
> Leader: *It was too hard to get it all done.*
>
> Boss: *And . . . what was hard?*

Leader explains the situation while boss listens without interrupting

Boss: *I understand it was hard and there were challenges.* (Reframe from team or individual problem to the bigger picture) *If it were easier, what would that be like for you?* (Refocus from negative to positive)

Leader: *Well, I have not thought about it in that way. Maybe we could . . .*

Boss: *From the idea of making it easier, what could you shift to get the project back on track?* (Redirect)

What about that client and their missing paperwork?

You: *I don't seem to have gotten the documents you were going to send me.* (Safe opening)

Client: *No, I didn't get all that done.*

You: *Okay.* (Pause) *No worries. I am curious. What do you want to happen going forward this next year?* (Reframe to the large picture)

Client: *I want to get this done by May.*

You: *How can we support you in doing this?* (Refocus)

Client: *I need to talk with my daughter about this . . . and I am not sure what to say to her.*

You: *Would you be willing to talk through how this might go right now?* (Redirect to action)

The conversation with your partner:

> You: *I understand you don't want to look at the new school for our kids; it is a different path than what we had planned.* (Reframe to reset conversation to other's interpretations)
>
> Partner: *Sure is, and you know I don't see the need right now.*
>
> You: *We don't have to decide right now. Would you be willing to just explore the option to see what is available?* (Refocus to the bigger picture)
>
> Partner: *Not sure about that.*
>
> You: *What if I get more information and we sit down together to look through it and decide the next steps to take?* (Redirect to action, with a nudge)

In each of these scenarios, there are many moving parts and subtle complexities. It is not always about solving the most apparent problem, but about using your skills to go deeper to help people explore what they are thinking and say what is on their minds. Instead of being stuck in *No,* or *We cannot do this*, you provide the opportunity to think it through. You can create a different conversational space to look beyond the obvious negative ideas, thoughts, or ways of doing things they may not have thought about before. You are planting seeds to bring in a different perspective and setting the stage for cocreating together.

This happens in real life. On October 26, 2018, in the World Series Game 3, the Boston Red Sox played the Los Angeles Dodgers in a grueling eighteen-inning, game lasting over seven hours that produced a loss for the Red Sox and drained them physically and mentally. The last pitch, from Boston's Nathan Eovaldi, was a home run for Max Muncy.

Red Sox Manager Alex Cora, who typically does not believe in team meetings, gathered his exhausted players for a meeting.

Cora began, "We just played one of the toughest games in World Series history. Red Sox. Dodgers. Dodger Stadium. World Series. We win together, we lose together. We do the best we can every day. And the way you competed is something all of us should be proud of. This is a great team. This was a great game. And you guys proved it tonight . . ."

When Cora was done, the room burst into a standing ovation. There were tears, and one by one, every player, coach, and staff member lined up to take turns hugging Eovaldi. *"Keep your eye on the ball, the series is ours."*

What did Cora do?

Reframed the game as a tough loss to how they all worked hard.

Refocused off the losing pitch to how great they were together.

Redirected by telling them how proud he was of them. That was epic and reminded them of the way back to the winning track.

The impact? Cora rallied the troops in his own way. He captured the room with one message for everyone that got them back on the winning page. While that game will be an all-time point of reference for baseball and the valiance of Eovaldi rising above all the striving, it was the appreciation and love of his teammates in the face of defeat that endures.

The Red Sox took the World Series in five games, their fourth World Championship in fifteen seasons.[30]

MAKE IT OR BREAK IT

Principle #5: Explore Meaning

1. Acknowledge the obvious and ask curious questions about their ideas to broaden perspectives, understand the situation, and put words to what they may be thinking and feeling.
2. Discover the roadblocks that get in the way of achieving their financial goals. Ask what different options could look like to them.
3. Connect them to the bigger picture of what they want.
4. Talk through and support them in how and where can they direct their attention right now for new opportunities. Don't tell clients *how it is* and expect that to be meaningful to them.

CHAPTER 11

Principle #6: Speak Up

Imagine you are in an important meeting to discuss a major initiative that did not work out as expected to see what else could be done. Previously, you had shared a couple ideas with your peers who encouraged you to bring them up. You're in the meeting and the time has come. You're feeling excited to share your ideas. They are right there on the tip of your tongue. But you pause, bite your tongue, and don't say anything.

Your memory is flooded with experiences—those crushing moments when you took the risk to voice your opinion and were met with criticism, judgment, or worse yet, you got no response at all. No one wants to say something and look ignorant or incompetent. You have given up on speaking up; it is not worth the risk.

People fear speaking up in conversations will lead to rejection. The feeling of rejection takes many forms and is as unique as the individual. It shows up in fearing that you will not be liked, and kicked out of the tribe. Fear that your ideas will not be heard or pushed under the rug, your importance minimalized. Fear that if you speak up there could be repercussions, punishment, or reprimand. The cost of people not speaking up is that there is miscommunication, misunderstanding, and conflict. Clients leave, employees leave, teams fail, parents fail, profitability fails. The best ideas, creativity, and innovation are left on the table.

When people do speak up in conversations, different ideas fuel creativity and act a catalyst to unlock deeper thinking. New ideas improve performance, creating solid strategies and alignment with decisions. It builds relationships and people feel part of the process. They know their opinions and contributions matter. They feel a part of the conversation where honesty and truthfulness are the norms, not the exception. Speaking up empowers people. It brings out the best in them.

The Science Of Silence

Our brain is always scanning for differences between how we see the world and what is actually showing up. Any difference in how we see the world and how others describe it triggers the brain to interpret those differences as a threat. This sets off an automatic biochemical response of fear, which changes our neural chemistry, automatically moving us into protection from perceived rejection.

When we put voice and words to these differences by actively and sincerely encouraging others to share how they see the situation, the brain opens up to listening to connect, to discovering of what they are saying, not criticism or judgment, and a mutual understanding is developed.

This understanding of others reduces the perceived threats and fear of rejection and gives permission to others to speak up and develop their opinions, thoughts, and feelings in conversations. Encoded in every conversation is the hidden language of trust. If there is not a level of trust, people are hesitant to say what is really on their minds. If you don't lead conversations where others can speak up, you won't gain trust and loyalty.

Amy Edmondson writes that where there is safety, there is trust. We can take the risk to say "I screwed up" or "I need help," as we know the people we work with will be supportive, direct, and honest to give candid feedback, openly admitting mistakes they have made so we can learn from each other. People can speak up without fearing rejection. This boosts engagement, innovation, learning from mistakes, and sharing of knowledge.[31]

Leading Empowering Conversations

It is through the quality of conversations you lead that others are encouraged to speak up with their ideas, opinions, and how they see things could work.

Leveraging what we know from science, there are specific conversational dynamics and skills to lead these conversations.

Role model empowering conversations. You must decide, as the leader of a conversation, that you want to be the kind of person who empowers people to speak up and your intention is to open up the conversational space and encourage others to voice their ideas.

As a leader, it is expected, whether working with your clients or team, that your responsibility is to set standards, direction, and strategy. There must be clarity with role definition, accountability, and metrics. You need to say what needs to be said, not always what others want to hear. But in the absence of a healthy dialog as to what that looks like, what that means for people, and how you accomplish this, you fail to develop people as thinking and learning human beings who can share their ideas. Instead, you have robots who do what they are told.

While others may fear speaking up, often even the leader fears speaking up. Leaders have been rewarded for being driven, ambitious, knowing what to do, and getting it done; their values and beliefs support this hard work and relentless drive.

However, leaders get triggered when challenges arise. They move to protection and self-preservation in the way they speak to others. In this protective mode, there is an underlying fear that if they open up the conversation to other ideas, time will be wasted since their way is best; all those ideas may get in the way of action, performance, and driving results. They fear that if they open up the conversation, they may not agree with the ideas. There is uncertainty in what to say when others disagree with their opinions or how to respond to a bad idea, a wild idea, or an idea that is not right for now.

With few facts, they jump right into problem-solving rather than problem-listening. They tell others what to do and use their position to influence others toward a particular action outcome or decision.

Actions speak louder than words. Show them by what you say and your actions that we all have the same human need to belong and to be connected. You no longer have to fear differences, as we have common ground. Make it a point to get to know them personally to strengthen emotional connection and bonding. Make a personal connection with others: greet people, smile, don't make them feel like they are an interruption.

Speak to bring forth your humanity. It may be easy to be transparent and talk about your experiences and situations. But when you bring in the emotion of how you were impacted and how you felt, transparency moves into vulnerability. It gets to the core of who you are, why you do what you do. Once you hear what people have gone through, you can never look at them the same way again. You start seeing them as people first, not a coworker or client. People start speaking to each other and feel comfortable sharing and being vulnerable with each other, sometimes for the first time.

Develop conversational norms. Establish guiding principles and standards for you, your team, and your clients in how you talk with each other and put into words what you can count on each other for in conversations.

- You can count on me to speak openly, knowing I don't have all the answers.
- You can count on me to explore and talk through options with you.
- You can count on me to meet deadlines and keep you up-to-date with progress.
- You can count on me to be respectful, fair, and honest.
- You can count on me to speak up, with care and candor, when these principles are not in play.

Invite engagement instead of being the expert. People instinctively understand that their fate lies in the hands of the higher-ups. Positional power pulls rank. If you are the boss, you have the power to fire me, pure and simple. If you are the service professional, you have power in your expertise and know what I don't know, which is why I have come to you. The emotional discomfort of speaking up and the fear of being scorned, ignored, or looking stupid in front on the higher-ups is so great that we go silent.

To develop others to find their voice, you must listen first and speak second. This can be a slippery slope. You may ask people to speak up, but when you don't hear the answer, you tell them what the answer is. This influences them to "follow the leader" and agree with your opinion and answers. You have to invite participation and that may mean asking people directly about their ideas. Listen carefully to their response to create that experience of genuine interest and safety.

Avoid the education trap. Out of your good intentions of generosity and kindness, you want to help other people get up to speed, shorten their learning curve, save them from making the dumb and costly mistakes you have made. Under the guise of educating others, you share your experiences and advise them what they should do. You already think you know what the other person is thinking and what they should do. You are not inviting them to speak up and have just fallen into the advising trap of telling and persuading. You moved into a conversation that shows them you know more, rather than developing the conversational space for others to speak up. People sense this and go silent.

Respond respectfully. Let them experience that you are open to influence by taking the risk to express your point of view. There is no language of right or wrong; it is just your viewpoint. Take the lead to make explicit that different points of view are welcome, respected, and will be heard. As you demonstrate speaking up, it sends the signal that you are giving them permission to speak up.

Fine-tune your ability to ask questions to convey that you are interested in them. Listening to what people are saying and building on their ideas or giving them feedback shows respect and reinforces the feeling that it is safe to speak up. It does not mean that you have to agree with them, but that you recognize and appreciate the effort it took to express themselves. It becomes a positive cycle of the more they trust, the more they feel safe, the more they contribute, the more self-confident they feel.

Encourage open and honest talk, and help others through your own words to disagree and challenge without being threatening. You teach them how to voice questions over different opinions, to debate rather than take things personally or fear backlash. You don't know everything and you don't have to do it alone; you can get a second opinion and let them know you value what they think.

When you stop yourself from telling, and instead welcome expression of all voices before deciding, you encourage pushback and give permission for others to chime in. I call that "poke holes in my thinking." "This is my opinion or idea, what do you think?" "That's an interesting idea. What if . . .?"

If you cannot use an idea, respond respectfully. Appreciate the effort it took to speak up to make a suggestion. Get curious and learn more about the idea. Set the context for why it may not be the current focus and when might be a better time. Clarify if and when you might be able to use this idea and how they can contribute. Sometimes, what seems like an idea you cannot use turns out to be brilliant and would not have been discovered if dismissed from the start. This role modeling inspires others to speak up about a good idea in the future.

Allow silence. People may go silent to internally process whether they can trust you and if they should speak up. They may be evaluating the situation, wondering what they will say next, or compare what you've said to what their own experiences have taught them.

You may get very uncomfortable with the silence since you don't know what others are thinking or feeling. Silence can create anxiety or be interpreted as rejection of what you said. And when the pause in the moment gets too much for us, we fill the space with idle conversation because it makes us feel better.

Silence is a gift and a mark of respect. It provides the space and opportunity for others to process what they are thinking, reflect longer, and think more deeply. If we wait it out and stop filling in the blanks for others, they will express what is on their minds.

Nudge people. People who are hesitant to speak up may speak up when given the opportunity and invitation directly or indirectly. There are a couple options to help them develop this skill.

You can call on others directly to share their thoughts by taking turns. But if this is not the conversational norm, it may back them into a corner and make them feel even more hesitant and fearful. Another option is to have a private conversation to let them know they have good ideas, talk through what holds them back, and ask how you can support them in speaking up.

You can ask others to contribute indirectly. Acknowledge that you sense some hesitancy, and when the time is right for them, you would like to hear from them.

Team Example

John was leading a team to develop different approaches to specific work processes. Each team member was given the assignment of coming up with one idea on how this might look. This particular meeting was about sharing different ideas of what could be possible.

John listened to a few ideas and then he could no longer contain himself and promptly announced, "While these are good ideas, they are ideas for another time. What we really need to do right now is . . ." He proceeded to persuade the group that his idea was the right one, "Of course you agree, don't you? Here is the plan on how to do it."

What do you think was the impact of this? Even though he meant well in getting things done "now," the impact on the team was that, even though others had good ideas, the likelihood of speaking up was squelched. The team thought John was running his own agenda and there was no room for other opinions.

Then John caught himself and the negative impact it was creating and stepped back into a do-over.

"I've just turned off the faucet of your ideas. I got so excited and passionate about this that I thought I had all the right answers. I sometimes forget what makes us great is choosing strategies based on what we *all* bring. Let's begin again so we can hear the rest of your ideas."

He sensed the tension and hesitancy to speak up. John called on each team member by name. He acknowledged a contribution they had made before and asked them to voice their ideas. By the end of the meeting, the team had a list of ideas, some for now, some for later, and the plan was cocreated.

The lesson that John learned was how easy it is to slip into conversations that are action oriented, that get results *now*. Level One and Two conversations do not get people on board and on the same page. With self-awareness and self-management of these trigger points, he could lead Level Three conversations that lessen fear and bring his team and organization together to foster appreciation and a growing sense of trust.

Leading masterful conversations in the face of differences of opinion, feedback, or performance challenges creates relationships based on trust. Thoughts, feelings, and opinions can be discussed openly without fear of recrimination, avoidance, or disapproval. As you speak up, you model conversational patterns that encourage others to do the same. These healthy conversations strengthen the relationship so trust can grow and flourish.

One More Question

As our conversations support our clients and team in developing their confidence to speak up, we must make sure we understand and don't second-guess or assume we know what they mean. And when we are not sure, or respectfully disagree, we need to tactfully speak the truth in what we hear. This prevents confusion, misalignment, and misunderstanding, and minimizes the perception that we were not listening when they took the risk to speak up.

We have previously discussed the skill and importance of how to ask questions for which you do not have the answer. This encourages the other person to speak up and answer how they understand a situation and how they see the world. People love talking about themselves since it triggers the reward feel-good state. It provides us with the clarity and understanding of how the other sees the world. It supports both of you in more fully understanding each other.

In responding to questions, many times people speak in terms of vagueness and generalities, such as "that was a great experience" or "that did not work out so well." We assume we know what they mean, as those words represent common experiences we have all had. But, the meaning of what was said is in the speaker's mind, not the listener's. As we listen, we think we understand what the words mean to us, but may miss out on specifically what the other was trying to convey.

When we hear these general terms, we ask one more question. We specifically ask what a word, phrase, or experience means to them. This is double-clicking. Double-clicking is like opening a folder on your computer. All of a sudden, not only did you find what you were looking for, there was so much more information there you had forgotten.

The same thing happens in conversation. Our brains hold a lot of information and memories in our long-term memory bank. This is healthy and prevents overload. When we ask people to describe what something means for them, double- clicking activates those stored meanings. They now have access to describing what they had forgotten about and now remember.

Try an experiment for one day: Listen for examples of general terms in conversations.

You did a good job; the results were good.

The project is coming along as expected.

Things are fine.

When that happens, double-click and ask one more question:

What made you feel it was a good job?

Describe for me what made the results good.

What specifically does coming along as expected mean?

What does that look like to you?

What's fine?

What else is going on?

You will be amazed at what details come forward to give you a better understanding of what they really mean.

Kristi's Story

I had a fabulous executive assistant who was a top performer except for one thing: she could not consistently get to work on time. In previous conversations, I laid down the law; why it was important, what she needed to do, and if she didn't, then firing would be on the horizon. Firing her for the one percent of the job she did not get right—which was my frustrated initial reaction—did not feel right; it made no sense. I decided to have a different kind of conversation with her to understand the real situation.

The next time the conversation came up, I double-clicked on her experience of getting to work on time. I listened to the other side of the story, her side. I started by asking what was going on that made it so difficult to be on time.

What I learned was that she was not irresponsible, as I had judged her to be; rather, she was incredibly responsible. She was getting three small kids to school and daycare and had a husband who traveled much of the time. Even though she had reliable backup, things happened at the last moment that delayed her. I got that. I flashed back to the one time I was fifteen minutes late in picking up my daughter from school. Standing there alone waiting for me, the first words out of her mouth were, "I thought you forgot me." I could empathize both with her feelings and the situation.

My first knee-jerk reaction was to make things better and compromise my standards. My second reaction was to lay the down law again, thinking *If I figured this out, so can you. Or maybe you are not responsible enough to have this job.*

Neither reaction felt right. Instead, I double-clicked on the words she used: "things could be different, this would improve." I then asked her different questions, "What needs to be different on your end? What do you see as possible solutions? What can I do to support you?"

That is when Kristi opened up. She had ideas all worked out; she had developed a plan with another executive assistant in the department with alternating start times that worked for both of them and for me. I learned that instead of giving up on the one percent that wasn't working and feeling obligated to make do, by understanding more thoroughly, we could make changes where we all won: a win for her and her counterpart, a win for me, and a win for the department.

As people are speaking up, *listen* to connect with what they are really saying.

Appreciate them for speaking up. Step into their experience with them. The mirror neurons activate empathy and they feel really comfortable with speaking up with what is on their minds and in their hearts.

The impact is that conversations do not stay at the surface level where we think we know what they are saying. It changes the understanding we have. Instead of getting off the track with what we think they mean, we get on track with having a deeper conversation to solve challenges differently.

Uncomfortable Conversations Are Inevitable

One of the least developed skills most of us have is the ability to speak up and lead difficult, challenging, or uncomfortable conversations. It stirs up negative emotions and threats to how we see and judge ourselves. We are afraid people will not like us, afraid they will say mean things about us to others that hurt our feelings, afraid they will discount the truth, afraid they will not take responsibility, afraid they will get angry and shift the blame to us.

It conjures up negative emotions, and judgments about how we see and judge the other person. They are difficult to talk with, and the conversation will probably go nowhere, as they are defensive, they will not listen; or they will feel guilty or fall apart, feel like they failed, feel embarrassed and disappointed, and think they are a bad person.

We have all been in the situation where someone screwed up. A project did not meet the deadline or someone failed to deliver on something they said they would. Office politics, stress levels, unmet expectations, and clashing personalities create the perfect setup for interpersonal conflicts to brew, whether in the workplace or with clients.

You know you have to have that difficult talk. You have avoided it long enough and are tired of walking on eggshells around them. You hope others don't notice, but you are hearing whispers from the grapevine. You are hoping it does not get worse before you are ready to have the talk. You spend a lot of time thinking about what you are going to say and when to have the talk. Meanwhile, you avoid not only having the talk, but that person. You don't make decisions as quickly as you could. You are exhausted.

Avoiding these conversations is a high price to pay, not only for you, but for other people involved; they cannot course-correct when they are not performing. When others see that performances are not managed, it sets the bar lower for everyone. Team members may wonder where they stand, and why you are not letting them know if they are missing the mark. They may wonder why they should give it their all when others just skate by. This reduces morale and productivity, and can lead to a toxic workplace and relationships.

Not having uncomfortable conversations has a huge economic impact. We may think of conflict as a confrontational fight—one wins and one loses. Fear of conflict is almost always a sign of trust problems. CPP Global Inc. estimates that employees at U.S. companies spend on average 2.8 hours a week in conflict.[32] Those are paid hours not actually working. It further lowers the standards for those performing, sets a culture of mediocrity, and gives the unwritten message that *we don't talk about that kind of thing here.*

Not having feedback conversations with clients based on your own fear and assumptions that if they don't speak up everything is good, limits developing yourself, correcting concerns, and enhancing your relationship. Price and Van Bortel surveyed affluent clients who left their advisor and the reasons for doing so.[33] Nearly nine out of ten clients said the investment management provided was actually good or even superior. The reason for leaving boiled down to how they were treated and the lack of attention and communication they received. Most advisors do not know as they do not ask.

This is why. Difficult is a word that triggers a perceived threat. It floods your brain with cortisol and limits access to the prefrontal cortex, the executive brain. Decision-making, strategy, problem-solving, connecting with others, and listening shut down. And if that is not enough, past experiences kick in and you literally cannot remember anything positive about having difficult conversations, let alone anything positive about the person in front of you. You get trapped into the default setting to fight to prove a point, sugarcoat the topic, avoid it completely and hope it will go away, or make nice and agree with whatever is said.

"If you wait long enough, difficult people either quit, retire or die. That's my management style."

Difficult Does Not Have To Be That Difficult

You can effectively transform a difficult, challenging, uncomfortable conversation to a learning, empowering conversation that builds a relationship. This allows people to come to terms with difficult situations, understand different points of view, and ensure decisions are well thought out. By working through uncomfortable conversations together, people become closer and trust others more. They know where they stand and what they can do moving forward. They can ask for help; and it's an opportunity for everyone—including the leader—to learn and grow, instead of walking on eggshells and hoping it will get better. It is likely everyone can feel happier and more satisfied with the work they do and their interactions with others. It creates a more inclusive environment. When people can dissent, debate, and speak up, they become more creative and productive.

The RESPOND Process

The RESPOND Process is a methodology that integrates science and how-to skills to lead uncomfortable conversations. These conversations are planned and designed. They don't happen by accident. Implementing a repeatable process and preparation move you from the uncertainty of *I don't know what to say or do* to knowing you can lead these conversations, even if they come up when you least except it, and sometimes they do. Your preparation is the key for a successful conversations.

This process applies to team members and clients. It applies to feedback, dealing with challenging topics, or addressing a misunderstanding that has reached the boiling point of a conflict.

Reframe from difficult to uncomfortable or learning conversation. Words matter. *Challenging, critical,* or *difficult* are trigger words that activate the fear response of avoidance and protection as your brain is running on cortisol. That decreases your ability to be open to listening, and to feel calm and confident.

When you shift the words you use, you shift your neural chemistry. It diffuses the fear state, signals the brain to be less reactive, and opens up the opportunity to make a new meaning and not get stuck. It calms anxieties and increases oxytocin to open up your executive brain.

Check your motives for this conversation before diving into the discussion. If your goal is to prove you are the smartest person in the room or dominate the conversation to feel superior, you are off track. It will only lead to defensiveness, misunderstanding, and dissolution of whatever tenuous trust you had.

Instead, prepare yourself with the perspective of a developmental opportunity to grow, learn, and improve. This supports you in being open and curious about how others see situations. You want the other person to leave the conversation knowing what they can do to improve, and that you treated them with respect and fairness.

Prepare yourself by asking:

What is my intention or purpose of this conversation?

What is the impact I want to create?

What is the outcome I want?

What do I want the other person to feel, think, or do differently after the conversation?

How do I want to show up in this conversation?

Explore the desired outcome. Discuss with the other person the roadmap of the conversation. Be clear about what you will talk about and why it is important. It sets the tone that you care enough to understand and address challenges honestly and openly. This allays anxiety and calms fear. The brain hates surprises and not knowing.

Share your intentions and what you hope will be gained by this conversation. People want to know where they stand. Sugarcoating does more harm than speaking the truth. "We are having this conversation because (specific situation). I have spent time thinking about it and want to understand what your (thoughts/feelings/views) on this are."

Share points of view. Make the conversation specific. Be clear about what you want to address, why it is important, and the impact it creates. Talk about one kind of issue or situation. Throwing out more than one issue gets confusing, diffused, muddled, and off course.

This requires you to be candid, open, honest, and nonjudgmental. "You were working on this (important project/client case). It was challenging in many aspects, and at end of this, the results were not what either one of us expected."

Discover their perspective first. You want to get a clear picture of what they think happened. "I would like to hear how this unfolded for you. What do you think worked well, and what did not?" This requires you to listen to connect to hear what they need to say, without judgment, correction, or rejection. Listen for the *meaning*, not a rebuttal. Listen for the feeling behind the words and empathize what it might be like to be them.

Share your perspective with candor, not with blame or accusations, but with clarity in what you know, what you think, and your viewpoint. People do not want to intentionally disappoint you, and usually know when their actions miss the mark. They feel embarrassed that they failed. Acknowledge that while this is difficult to hear, the goal is growing in their skills and abilities.

Don't rush through it. Honest conversations address uncomfortable truths, so take the lead in being direct and kind. Because these conversations can be uncomfortable, our brains trigger us in two different ways. One is a tendency to race through these conversations to escape them and get them over with. The second is to talk on and on while not much of that applies to the topic at hand. Give the specifics of the situation in a few sentences. It is then your turn to listen and understand the other person's perspective. Slow down and take into consideration the human being sitting across from you.

Probe further. The difference between how you understand the issue and how the other person sees things creates a gap. Make sure there is mutual understanding and a clear definition of the cause of the issue and the impact created.

The words you use are important. Avoid using generic terms like *attitude, always, never*. They provide no concrete context or behavioral cues to what you are talking about. These terms trigger people into defending themselves, not addressing the issue at hand.

Manage the emotional and contextual discussion at hand. Emotions can run high and it is important that you acknowledge this and allow others to compose themselves. If they blame you, acknowledge that may be how they see things, but refocus the conversation on them and the specifics you set up.

Ask questions for which you do not know the answers. For further clarification, understanding, and definition of the problems ask, "What were the circumstances that led you down this path?" or "What experience did you have that was different?"

Ownership. Be clear about the role each of you play. Avoid taking responsibility that is not yours or assigning responsibility outside of the scope of what the other can do. When the dots are connected between actions and impact, we move to understanding the interdependence of the situation.

Leading conversations is not a monologue of who is right or just telling others what went wrong and how to fix it. It is a dialogue to understand, problem-solve, and move forward. The supportive tone and working together attitude, rather than blame, helps alleviate fears and negative feelings the other person has. It decreases your feelings of responsibility to change someone—which you know you cannot do, but somehow think it is your job. When both parties speak up, options and solutions to move forward are cocreated from the best of ideas by both. This develops people.

Needs. There is no misbehavior, only unmet needs. Get to the core of what the unmet needs are. People do things for a reason. Discover why they do what they do, and why they *want* to do the things you want them do. You cannot make someone do anything. You cannot compel them to do anything.

Is there a knowing and doing gap? Knowing is not doing.

> *Do they know how to do what you have asked?*
>
> *Do they have the resources?*
>
> *Do they know the priorities?*
>
> *Do they want to do this? Maybe they are going through a rough patch in life and do not have the mental energy. The question is, do you want to support them through this?*

Some people just may not be the right fit based on their needs. If they aren't, you may need to help them find a different resources.

Develop The Plan. Focus on the future so this becomes a learning opportunity. It needs to be specific, measureable, and written. Contract for success using constructive foresight:

> *What needs to happen for this to be successful in the future?*
>
> *Specifically, what will each of you contribute to this?*
>
> *How will you measure this?*
>
> *When and how will you evaluate progress?*
>
> *What will each of you do if the changes are not working?*

Before you move on, double confirm you are on the same page.

Samantha And The Dream Client Using The RESPOND Methodology

Samantha received a referral from one of her top clients. The client shared with Samantha that she did such good work with her friend, she should "just put together the plan that we talked about and I will sign off."

Samantha thought this seemed too easy. She sent preliminary documents to the client to discuss at their next meeting. Samantha then received a curt voice mail from the new client saying, "What you did was all wrong. We have got to talk about this and I will see you this afternoon."

Samantha's initial reaction (what she really was thinking to say in the heat of the moment) was: *She doesn't know what she wants. I should have known this case would be trouble; it was too easy. When we meet, I am going to tell her I did exactly what she asked.*

Samantha used the RESPOND process and this is how the conversation developed.

Reframe: She prepared and changed her intention for the client meeting from blame and judge this as a bad client to understand and learn what was not clear in how they are working together.

Explore: Samantha: "Before we begin, it seems there is something I don't understand. You wanted me to put this plan together so you could sign off. Your voicemail said that something was wrong. Let's talk about this so I better understand what's going on."

Share: Client: "I thought that you would prepare this, we would review it, and then I would sign off on it, but not in an email. Besides, my best friend, a CPA who retired 15 years ago, took a look at this and said it was all wrong. You did not consider the tax implications and I would be on the hook for a lot more than I bargained for."

Probe: Samantha: "I appreciate your willingness to share that. The point of the preliminary documents was for your information and as a springboard for our discussion. It seems like there is a misstep here in understanding each other.

"I assumed you knew that these were preliminary documents. The next steps would be to talk through these, answer questions and address issues like the tax implication. You assumed that I expected you to sign off on the spot. Am I getting this accurately?"

Client: "That is not what I thought you said. I don't remember you telling me that."

Ownership: Samantha: "It seems like there is a misstep here in understanding each other. I apologize if I did not clearly explain this. When we work together you can call us, me or someone on my team, anytime concerns come up."

Needs: Samantha: "What is most important to you as we work together?"

Client: "I just need to know that we can talk through things, that you will help me to decode all this stuff I don't know about or care to manage myself . . . and that you will be there. Like that tax thing; I was worried you were not on top of it. Something about paying more taxes that I don't understand."

Samantha: "What I need you to do is to talk with me openly, like you are doing, when these things come up. We'll address them right away so you don't have to sit and wonder."

Develop the plan: Samantha: "What needs to shift so we can both be on the same page?"

And the conversation continued back and forth. In just a few minutes, they worked out together how to communicate and what was important for the client–advisor relationship to be successful. They defined their relationship and way of doing business together. The client indeed became a dream client and has referred many more new clients along the way.

Speaking Up During Client Conversations

People seek out professionals such as financial services advisors, attorneys, doctors, teachers, or coaches because they need their guidance for a particular matter or to reach a goal. They defer to your suggestions. They don't speak up because they assume you have their best interests at heart. If they did challenge your expertise, they may fear it would hurt the relationship.

We cannot overlook the importance of giving timely feedback to clients. If you do not do this, they wonder if they can really trust you. If they are making poor decisions that do not align with their goals, does your fear of speaking up and possibly damaging the relationship keep you silent and agreeing with them? Giving relevant feedback when you see a contradiction is an opportunity. It actively shows you care enough to ask for their opinions and offer guidance. This facilitates a relationship based on trust and respect.

Asking your clients for feedback is one of the biggest missed opportunities. We assume they will let us know if something is amiss. We assume if there are concerns about something that somehow we have failed. So we don't speak up and just go along, assuming our clients are satisfied. But satisfied clients are not necessarily engaged clients, connected clients, or clients who will stay with us.

At the close of every meeting, there is an opportunity to ask for feedback. You are not fishing for how great you are, but giving permission to your clients to speak up about their experience—including what they may have been dissatisfied with or what you could have done better in service of them. It shows you care. Your clients will feel respected and valued. They will know they matter.

It is as simple as asking a few questions to discover more about their experience. *What did we not address that you had hoped we would cover? What are you feeling uncertain or unsure about? What was most helpful to you? What were your key learning or take-aways? Where could we have done better?*

If we don't encourage others to speak up or avoid speaking up ourselves and having those uncomfortable conversations, petty misunderstandings, power struggles, and differences of opinions can become the breeding ground for unhealthy relationships. While there is no such thing as a conflict-free workplace or relationship, we can lead uncomfortable conversations that encourage people to speak up and resolve differences—which builds stronger, healthy relationships.

How you lead conversations to encourage others to speak up can make or break a relationship. Thoughts, feelings, and opinions can be discussed without fear of recrimination, avoidance, or disapproval. Verbalizing how to work out challenges, problems, and issues as they arise strengthens the relationship. It transforms fear into trust, whereby you learn, grow, and develop yourself while empowering others to speak up, be heard, and work together.

MAKE IT OR BREAK IT

Principle #6: Speak Up

1. Uncomfortable conversations are inevitable, but making them difficult is optional. Effective uncomfortable conversations are designed; they are not accidental.

2. Make a decision that you want to lead conversations that empower people to speak up. Encourage your clients to share their point of view.

3. Perceptions of differences automatically trigger a fear response. Open up the conversation to understand and acknowledge the differences instead of assuming everyone looks at the world the way you do.

4. Listen first, speak second. Provide the space and interest for what your clients think and feel, and acknowledge them and what they have to say.

5. Pay attention to and never dismiss the personal and emotional aspects of financial decision-making.

6. Give your clients permission to speak up and invite feedback on their experience with you.

CHAPTER 12

Principle #7: Success Together

Humans have the need and desire to connect. This feeling of being close and connected to others involves feeling loved, cared for, and valued—and forms the basis of our relationships.[34] The quality of our conversations validate the invisible emotion of connection, allowing us to bond with each other to build and grow meaningful relationships.

Success together conversations put into words the experience of our human connectedness. It is the ability to share with others the past, present, and how we can be a part of shaping the future. Recognizing, appreciating, and celebrating our everyday experiences and accomplishments connects us not just to each other, but to how we contribute to a community that is bigger than ourselves.

One of the biggest opportunities leaders may be missing is to regularly communicate success together though their recognition, appreciation, and celebration of others. When this is shared publicly, it boosts client and team engagement, enhances loyalty, and increases productivity and retention by sending a clear message of how we are successful together.

Gallup concludes that only one in three employees strongly agree that they have received recognition in the past week.[35] People feel they are just another cog in the wheel of the machine getting the work done. When challenges and changes arise, as they do constantly, they put their heads down and buck up, because if they don't, someone else will. Or, they may harbor silent resentments only to surface as off-handed comments and water cooler talk. They certainly are not doing their best, giving their best, or bringing the best of themselves to work.

Appreciation also impacts client relationships. As cited earlier, Prince and Van Bortel discuss that when high net worth clients who have been working with you for years leave, it is usually because of communication. Clients who are rushed or feel unheard often think the advisor isn't providing value and lacks understanding of what is important to them. That translates to *you don't care*. They may come for technical expertise, but they stay or leave because of the relationship connection you have with them.

This is true in every industry or profession. When people leave or check out—whether clients, staff, or family—there is one indicator that holds true: we aren't communicating our appreciation of them. It is much easier to find fault, blame, criticize, or talk down to them than it is to be open and vulnerable enough to say, *you count and what you do matters*. Results of metrics, while tangible and important, are overshadowed by the dynamics of how we got there—how we worked together and counted on each other to create the numbers. How we did this is what counts.

We must learn how to have conversations today that share success and appreciation of others now. The future of work is creating learning businesses and learning people. A Deloitte study that looked at the top ten trends for the next ten years found that developing people requires learning, unlearning, and relearning. These behaviors drive performance when aligned with individual, team, and business goals.[36] Sharing success is critical to facilitate this learning process.

When we notice the people who helped us out, learn how they reached their milestones, and talk about what they did to reach their goals and accomplishments, we can learn together. It becomes the catalyst to look at what we are doing and question if there are different ideas we have not thought about.

Leading Conversation That Share Success; What Is Made Together, Stays Together

Success together happens through conversation: knowing where we are going, what's important to me, what's important to you, and how to navigate this together.

Going in for a routine dental appointment, I saw my regular dentist, who I had been with for years. I was satisfied; he did good work as far I could tell—my teeth were not falling out and I didn't need any work. But almost like clockwork, at the end of every appointment came the criticism and lecture. "You need to do more flossing. This baby tooth is okay but might need some work; better to do it sooner than later. Schedule your next six-month appointment, and we will work on that baby tooth."

Can you imagine how I felt leaving that office? I felt scolded, that no matter what I did, it still could be better, and then I was upsold on a problem that really was not urgent. That baby tooth had been with me since age six and is still doing fine! While I had been putting up with this lecture for years, on that particular day, I was done with it. That conversation broke our relationship.

The next dental appointment I had was with a new dentist. Expecting pretty much the same treatment, I was pleasantly surprised. The conversation started with, "I'm happy to get to know new clients," and proceeded to, "You are taking great care of your teeth, especially that baby tooth. What do you do?" That one comment opened up the entire conversation. I asked that even though there was no urgency, what if something happened? Would I be walking around with this gaping hole in my mouth? I was kindly given several options for the future, and if something did happen, they would be there to walk me through it.

Can you imagine how I felt leaving that day? It felt so good! That one comment of appreciation and a plan for success together made our relationship. The work I had been doing was recognized, I was given a few options along the way, and there with no upselling or urgency scare.

A few weeks later, I called them for an unrelated matter. "My daughter wants an orthodontist referral for her son. Who is as good as you are when it comes to caring for patients?"

You may wonder why I am telling you this. What does a dentist have to do with you, the financial planner or leader, and what you do?

These professionals knew exactly what to say and do to create shared success and they did it as a matter of their everyday conversation. In forty-five minutes, they transformed a new customer to a loyal client who feels connected to them and sees them as a partner.

What did the new dentist do?

Led conversations that verbally acknowledged the effort I was putting in.

Showed curiosity as to what I was doing to get there.

Uncovered worries I had about the future of that baby tooth and being toothless.

Shared how we could work together and how they would be there if something should happen.

What did my former dentist do?

Just stuck to the facts.

Told me the changes I needed to make.

Told me what "urgently" needed to be done, but it was not so urgent we couldn't take care of it in six months.

The Science Of Partnerships

Human beings thrive on defining what success looks like to them and celebrating success with others to mark their progress. But many times, we think the most important thing is the bottom line, getting things done, and deadlines. That breaks a relationship every time.

What makes a relationship? When we develop a common view of success and what that means, it allows us to build trust, make decisions, and work out differences fairly.

To develop loyal clients deeply connected to you, you must lead conversations that celebrate the effort they are putting in, and share in their progress of reaching their milestones and goals no matter how big or small; they all count. Supporting them and making meaningful decisions together (with you as their guide) will propel them to their aspirations and beyond.

We have mirror neurons, located below the prefrontal cortex, the executive brain. When we feel that others appreciate us and respect us, the mirror neurons are activated and oxytocin is released. These neurons facilitate connection and shared meaning, which reinforces trust. Through conversations, a link is developed far beyond what we can perceive from the outside. It is like the brain waves begin to match each other.

Have your ever experienced this?

- In a conversation, the other person said what was just on the tip of your tongue.
- You met someone new and you just clicked; you had that instant connection.
- Maybe you don't remember exactly what someone said, but how they made you feel changed the course of your life.

Princeton neuroscientist Uri Hasson peers into people's brains using an MRI to see what happens in everyday conversations. He uncovered something fascinating when two people connect: When we relate on a deep level, our brain activity mirrors the others. The stronger the connection—the more we "clicked"—the more our brain scans mirror each other, like they are synchronizing to allow a connection. The stronger the connection between the speaker and listener, the better the understanding.[37]

Conversational Practices To Include In Every Conversation

When we share success, there is a brain-to-brain coupling with the other person. When we embed this concept of shared success into everyday conversations, we feel connected, engaged, and can shape the future. We are in sync.

Acknowledge others with a general comment, short phrase, and appropriate gesture to support social distancing. It lets the other person know you are listening, paying attention, and interested in their success and milestones. You have experienced comments such as:

- Good job
- Well done.
- You are making progress.

While these comments are a start, and they feel good in the moment, they are quickly lost as there is little emotional resonance.

Appreciate others with emotion attached to it, to leave a memorable moment. This activates the prefrontal cortex, signals they are not alone, and they can count on you to notice the effort they are putting in. Take the above comments and add emotion to have a different impact:

- Good job. I appreciate you sticking with our plan.
- Well done. Your openness to talk about what is really going on, the changes you are going through, make it easier for us to move forward. Thank you.

- I admire your making decisions and progress in adjusting to what's going on in your world right now.

Aspire with others by connecting the dots between their hopes and dreams with your continued support, guidance, and partnership. Help them to understand they are getting where they want to go. Your eye is always on the horizon and tapping into something that is bigger than just the immediate:

- We are getting there together.
- I am honored to be a part of your journey and working together.
- Your big goals/dreams/aspirations of (retirement/ sending kids to college/getting that big promotion) may seem like they are far away, but everything we are doing together counts toward getting there.

What Does Success Mean And Look Like To Your Client?

To share success together, we must first understand what that means to the other. Have you ever asked your client to describe what an ideal client relationship would be like? Most people don't. We go along assuming things are fine. We make the dangerous assumption that we know what they want. We miss the opportunity to set the stage for cocreating and sharing success as milestones are met.

There are four questions I ask whenever I meet with current clients regarding a change in direction; a decision to be reached; or a new project, innovation, or strategy they want to implement. I also ask loved ones questions when they are in the midst of decision-making and seek advice.

1. What does success look like to you? (Double-click for clarity and specificity.)
2. What will that give you?
3. What will happen when you do this?
4. What impact will that have?

It creates the conversational space that allows them to consider and clarify what they want and what it will look like for them. It opens up the doors of possibility and engages their prefrontal cortex for bigger thinking. It gives me the opportunity to listen deeply, connect with them and their aspirations, and set the stage for a relationship where we can both bring our best. We are in this together.

What Does Shared Success Look Like For Your Team?

Looking back to look forward is another way to create shared success. When we see where the company or firm is going, the brain looks back to what it did before and what it is doing now, and then looks into the future, wondering, "How can I make it better than the present?"

Here are some questions to ask before you end team conversations. Keep it simple and brief and remember it's about being aware of and proactive with concerns to remedy them and clarify anything that was not understood.

What did you like about our meeting?

What do you want to explore further?

Did anything cause you to feel anxiety? Worry? Unsettled?

What can we do to address this now so you don't worry about it?

Where could we have done better?

What would you like to discuss at our next meeting?

Opening conversations to *what ifs* and sharing success can be frightening and exhilarating at the same time—frightening because we fear criticism and judgment. We have been told many times to just follow the rules, stay in line, or "this is how we do things around here." So, we go along to get along and are compliant, but underneath, there may be uncertainty, fear, and resentment.

Sharing success can be exhilarating because we focus on working together, which increases oxytocin and the sense of connection. When people feel that they listen differently and grow in new directions. When their opinions are asked for and acknowledged, they bond, get into sync, and develop partnerships.

When we share what success looks like, we also notice and acknowledge how we all are different. Certain people are thinkers, others are doers. We are not better than, or more talented than, or smarter than. We have different talents and gifts. We have different ideas on how to get there. When people operate differently than we do, resistance and disengagement set in. We categorize, label, and judge people.

When we acknowledge that we are not all alike, we can use shared success as a way to use these differences to appreciate that while we have different ways in working, we share a common bond in working toward the goal. The more we understand what each brings, the more helpful we can be to each other. When people know and feel they have others to count on, oxytocin flows and trust develops. With this trust, our brain acts differently. We are smarter, have integrity, develop strategy, and feel empathy and compassion. That's how we success together connects us.

Sharing success through acknowledgment and appreciation is so much more than donuts, a pizza party, or client events. We enjoy that donut or pizza in the moment, but it is gone quickly. And as quickly as we ate it, the feeling of success goes with it. Capture the essence of mutual success together through using words and emotions that describe milestones, leaving a lasting memory and positive experience.

We share success together, we work together, we are in sync. That level of connection and trust that we develop through our conversations makes our relationships.

> *"I have learned that people will forget what you said, people will forget what you did, but people will never forget how you made them feel."*
>
> —Maya Angelou

MAKE IT OR BREAK IT

Principle # 7: Success Together

1. Ask your clients and team to define what success looks like to them.
2. Acknowledge, appreciate and verbally celebrate progress and milestones with your clients and team.
3. Don't just stick to the business at hand. Connect the dots between your partnership with them in achieving their aspirations.
4. Never be too busy to notice and talk about what's worth celebrating. No matter how big or small—it all counts.

EPILOGUE

Axel And The Purple Lipstick

To recap, every conversation we have can either make or break a relationship. The levels of conversation we use either moves people into protection or connection. While your intention may be positive, the impact of the conversation and the interactions that develop may not be.

Every interaction we have leaves a lasting impression. The brain stores conversational patterns and interactions, influencing how people will feel about talking with you in the future. *Every conversation matters.*

To remind you of the lessons of this book, here is a true story about my five-year-old grandson Axel and how conversations can get derailed.

It was 2015 and we were at Macy's department store. The one and only thing we had to do before we got to the adventures of the day was to go with Mommy to exchange her lip gloss for a different color. I said I'd keep an eye on both kids while she did. It would only take a minute.

From a distance, we all saw the Chanel display at once. There it was . . . big, bright, colorful, beautiful, and oh so tempting to explore. Counter upon counter of bottles of all sizes and shapes. Rows and rows of exciting colors, tubes of different shapes, powder compacts, colored pencils, different liquids, jars of all sizes. Sort of looks like the Crayola store to kids.

All of a sudden, my sweet, sensitive, dearest grandson broke free from holding my hand and headed toward the lipstick counter at a full run looking like a little madman. With my other hand still holding his sister Juliet's hand, we quickly followed him. I called, "Wait up. We're right behind you."

Axel glanced back at us and continued full speed ahead with this devious smile that clearly signaled his mischievous, defiant thoughts. *Just try to stop me!* his eyes exclaimed.

In the few seconds it took us to reach Axel, he had already proudly grabbed a tube of purple lip gloss and emphatically declared, "Look, I have purple! And I am putting it all over my face!"

In that moment, my skin went very hot and white. Part of me was mortified that he would behave like this at the Chanel counter, of all places! Did he not know or care that there were people watching and judging us?

We are not the "kind of people" who don't control their children. We have well-behaved children, not ill-behaved wild monsters.

The other part of me was exploding with rage. *Why can't you just act like the sweet little boy you are?*

My memory flooded back to previous moments and times. *He is not an ill-behaved demon, but a soft, sweet, red-cheeked, cherubic, innocent child. I remember holding him in my arms, feeling his warm snuggle, gazing into his hazel eyes, and feeling such joy about how much I loved him and how I was thrilled to be part of his growing up years. I imagined all of the hopes and dreams his life would unfold. I get to see this and be part of it!*

As I got closer to him, I did not see the sweet little boy. I saw a little demon that I had to get under control before he made me look the fool in one of my favorite stores. The rules for belonging to this Exclusive Chanel Club—this top-notch, brand-exclusive group—were that we all were powerful, well-groomed, well-behaved women, a bit hoity-toity, and at our peak of perfection. We were *not* chasing after some ill-behaved, uncontrollable, five-year-old wild child.

"You are *not* putting that all over your face," I insisted fiercely. "Did you hear me, Axel? You are *not*." I held out my hand. "Give that back to me right now. It is not yours; it belongs to the store. It is for the women here, not for boys to create war paint. Besides, all of these strangers have touched it and it has germs all over it."

Well done, I thought. *I got the point across loud and clear. Who does this child think he is, trying to outsmart* me *with all of my logic and reason?*

After I had delivered this power directive, I looked Axel in the eyes, expecting a compliant giving over of the purple lip gloss.

But he thought otherwise.

It was the squinty eyes, furrowed eyebrows, and devilish smile that gave me the clue that this conversation was going absolutely nowhere. His entire expression dared me to just try and make him hand it over.

It didn't help that his sister was clapping and laughing with obvious delight, just imagining what was about to happen.

In my mind's eye, I saw it: This crazy Mary woman breathing fire out of her nostrils (but still looking good by Chanel standards) chasing after this adorable little boy while his darling sister provided applause, cheering him to run faster. Fire-breathing Grandmother Mar-Mar yelling, screaming, and threatening like a madwoman to stop it. She would finally reach him after chasing him all through the store aisles, tackling . . . no, *crushing* him with her power. She would win! Horrified bystanders wouldn't know if they should call 911's mental health team, child protection services, or just run out of the store and pretend none of it ever happened.

I shook my head. *No, no, that won't do.*

Before he had the chance to run away from my powerful grip, I firmly grabbed his tiny waist and planted him in the luxurious makeup chair, right next to the purple lip gloss display.

I need to set this situation straight.

Taking a deep breath to control my rage, I said in the most soothing voice I could muster: "Axel, honey, all you need to do is what I tell you. Give me that damn (yes, I even used potty language to make my point) purple lip gloss and everything will be fine."

I got this covered. Situation solved. I am smarter than this boy. Years of negotiation, well-tuned logic, and reason will save the day. Nothing embarrassing is going to happen on my watch! Besides, there is no more perfect person than a grandmother to straighten a child out, just a little bit.

Out of nowhere, I suddenly froze. It's like my entire body stopped and I felt it. (The hijack.) That feeling you get when you are dreaming and feeling like you are falling, falling, falling into nowhere, only to wake up and find yourself firmly and safely grounded in your bed.

It was like a switch flipped on. The lightning bolt of curiosity hit me and shook me to the core.

What is wrong with you, Mary? Why would you want to crush this beautiful child? He is full of spirit and energy and his big job right now, maybe even his mission in life, is to discover, to explore, to figure out his own power.

I shuddered, *Oh, my god. Look, I was getting ready to do to him what was done to me! My conditioned response and the chemical cocktail in my brain makes me want to act just like this demon five-year-old. But I have more maturity and life experience, and hopefully, am wiser that that.*

From this point of view, I could make a different choice.

I can feel strong, powerful, in control. I can be the authority who knows it all and makes this little boy feel stupid, ashamed for his curiosity, and feeling like a bad boy who is not worth much. (Of course, on the outside he will behave around me, but probably not like me too much.) It would be a slow death by intimidation that lasts a lifetime.

I shook my head at the horror.

I will choose the other path. I will find humor in his curiosity and help channel and direct his energy so that he can learn; make his own decisions; and grow into the strong, gracious, sensitive, caring young man that I am already seeing. I am thrilled to be part of his growing up, to experience his hopes and dreams, and get to be a part of all of this, just as I felt that day when I was gazing into the eyes of this innocent child on his first day on the planet.

So I slowly and carefully, but with deep resolve, approached Axel.

"Axel, show me that tube of lip gloss you are holding."

Reluctantly, and with a grip so tight his knuckles were turning white, he gave me a brief glimpse at it, and quickly returned his hand to his safe, secret hiding place deep inside his coat pocket.

I am sure the fear of God is in him that I will not only pry this precious tube out his tiny little hands and take it away forever, but that he will also get the lesson with all my powerful big words like "bad behavior," "you know better," and "you are smarter than this."

I squatted down so we were eye to eye and quietly asked him, "What makes this lip gloss so important to you?"

Axel perked up in the makeup chair and gave me a charming smile that told me how grateful he was to be asked this question.

"Mommy puts lip gloss on all the time. I know she likes the color purple and I wanted to show her that I found her favorite color. Just for Mommy."

I gently place my hands on his knees and looked into those beautiful hazel eyes.

"Wow! Oh, I think I get it now. You are so proud that you discovered this color just for Mommy and want to share your special surprise with her . . . right?"

He nodded.

"You are the kindest five-year-old I know. I love that about you, and I love you." I made sure he saw and felt all the love I had for him in that moment. "Now, I've got an idea on how you can really surprise Mommy. Wanna hear about it? And maybe you won't even have to put the lip gloss all over your face."

"Yeah!" His eyes lit up and the demon was gone.

"To try it on, most people put it here on their wrists to get an idea of the color. Can I show you?" I asked as I pointed to the underside of his wrist.

"Okay!" he exclaimed as he held out his wrist.

When I put the purple lip gloss on his wrist, he smiled with delight. "I love the color, and Mommy will, too."

He jumped out of the chair and ran to his mother, so eager to share his latest discovery, one made just for her.

I think to myself how precious that moment was, but almost wasn't.

The Moral Of The Story

The purple lip gloss is a shining example of everyday situations where we get to choose the kind of conversation we want to have—to determine whether we are building relationships with a foundation of trust or distrust. You can either build distrust with power, influence, and telling others what to do, or lead conversations that build trust by connecting and seeking to understand.

APPENDIX A

Acknowledgments

A debt of thanks to the following:

Judith E. Glaser, my mentor, who generously shared her life work through teaching others how the unique combination of science and skills cocreate powerful conversations that build trust. Parts of the content presented are adapted from Conversational Intelligence ® and her work.

Bob Klefsaas, CEO, All Star Financial, for his vision and thought leadership to build a holistic fee-only wealth management firm in 1987, one of the first in the state of Minnesota. The firm's core values of putting the client at the center of everything and doing the right thing keeps he and his team at the forefront of redefining the future of client-advisor relationship.

My valued partners/friends on the All Star Team, who by working with me cocreated the Conversational Edge Program: Brian Senske, J. Alexander Kallebo, Matt Berhow, Sam Sexton, David Osterberg, Brady Mickolichek, Paula Zilka, Nicole VandenPlas, Kaitlin Buckley, Lucelia Husby, and Zhaoren Chen. They lead everyday conversations with one purpose in mind and that is to serve their valued clients, each other, their families, friends, and community.

I have been privileged to have the friendship, encouragement, and candor from clients and colleagues who themselves are transforming their industry conversations. These conversational change makers include Joan Giles, Michelle Klisanich, Mike Schweitzer, Kevin and Nikki Erickson, Kathryn Cashman, Deirdre Van Nest, and Mike Schmid.

Mark LeBlanc, my coach, who encouraged taking one next step, and gave me courage to write "that book that is within you." Which led me to my faithful editor and publisher Henry DeVries, who patiently and kindly was with me every step of the way. He embodies living in integrity and has shown me that everything we do in marketing can be done with invitation and generosity.

My family—daughter Jana, her partner Kent, and my inquisitive, truth-seeking grandchildren, Axel and Juliet—who have taught me the most important lesson of all. We are family. We are all connected. We make conversations, which are the glue to family, business, and life.

APPENDIX B

About The Author

Mary Schmid, MBA, runs a Minnesota-based speaking and consulting business. She believes everything begins with a conversation to build relationships. The key to building healthy relationships is knowing what makes or breaks a conversation. When you learn the science of what goes on in the brain in every conversation, you can learn the skills of how to lead conversations that earn trust.

Her model is for financial professionals and their teams who want to lead high-trust conversations and build relationships that last. Her clients often share that they can focus conversations on what matters to their clients and team and have a higher degree of confidence in what to say in the moment, allowing the people they work with to feel heard, understood, and satisfied every time they interact.

On a personal note, when she is not out speaking or training, you might find Mary on a travel adventure with her family. To contact Mary regarding bulk orders of this book, working with your team, or speaking at your next event, go to www.MarySchmid.com or call 612-964-6002.

APPENDIX C

References

Balboa, Nicklas and Richard D. Glaser, Ph.D. "The Neuroscience of Conversations." *Psychology Today* (May 2019).

Baumeister, Roy F. and Mark R. Leary. "The Need to Belong: Desire for Interpersonal Attachments as a Fundamental Human Motivation." *Psychological Bulletin* 117, no. 3 (1995): 497-529.

Brown, Brene. *Daring Greatly*. New York, NY: Penguin Random House, 2012.

Brown, Brene. *Rising Strong*. New York, NY: Penguin Random House, 2015.

Dalio, Ray. *Principles*. New York, NY: Simon and Schuster, 2017.

Dimoka, Angelika. "What Does the Brain Tell Us About Trust and Distrust? Evidence from a Functional Neuroimaging Study." *Management Information Systems Quarterly,* 34 (2010).

Edmondson, Amy and Kathryn Roloff. "Leveraging Diversity Through Psychological Safety." *Rotman Magazine* (2009).

Edmondson, Amy. "Psychological Safety and Learning Behavior in Work Teams." Administrative Quarterly 44, no. 3 (1999):350-383.

Eisenberger, Naomi I. and Steve W. Cole. "Social neuroscience and health: neurophysiological mechanisms linking social ties with physical health." Nature Neuroscience (2012).

Eurich, Tasha. "What Self Awareness Really Is." *Harvard Business Review* (January 2018).

Flaum, J.P. "When it Comes to Business Leadership, Nice Guys Finish First." *Green Peak Partners* (2010). http://greenpeakpartners.com/wp-content/uploads/2018/09/Green-Peak_Cornell-University-Study_What-predicts-success.pdf

Ghosh, Prarthana. "The Future of Work: 10 Key Trends for the Next 10 Years." *HR Technologist* (July 2019).

Gino, Francesca. "The Business Case for Curiosity." *Harvard Business Review (September-October* 2018).

Glaser, Judith. *Conversational Intelligence*. Brookline, MA: Bibliomotion, Inc., 2014.

Glaser, Judith. "Why You're Talking Past Each Other, and How to Stop." Harvard Business Review (December 2012).

Goleman, Daniel. *Emotional Intelligence: Why It Can Matter More Than IQ*. New York, NY: Bantam Books, 1995.

Goleman, Daniel. *Working with Emotional Intelligence*. New York, NY: Bantam Books, 1998.

Green, Mitchell, "Speech Acts", The Stanford Encyclopedia of Philosophy (Winter 2017 Edition), Edward N. Zalta (ed.), https://plato.stanford.edu/archives/win2017/entries/speech-acts/.

Hargie, Owen. Skilled Interpersonal Interaction: Research, Theory, and Practice. London: Routledge, 2017.

Lencioni, Patrick. *The Five Dysfunctions of a Team*. San Francisco, CA: Jossey-Bass, 2002.

Lieberman, Matthew D. *Why Our Brains Are Wired to Connect*. New York, NY: Crown Publishers, 2013.

Littlechild, Julie. Investments and Wealth Institute Special Report, 2020 Investor Research, "The Current Crisis, The Impact on Client Loyalty, and the Implications for Your Business."

Mann, Ann Marie and Nate Dvorak. "Employee Recognition: Low Cost, High Impact." *Gallup Workplace* (June 2016).

Maxfield, David. "How a Culture of Silence Eats Away At Your Company." *Harvard Business Review* (December 2016).

Medina, John. *Brain Rules*. Seattle, WA: Pear Press, 2014. "New Client Research Uncovers Drivers of Engagement, Satisfaction, and Willingness to Refer." Investment and Wealth Management. Research, 2019. https://www.prweb.com/releases/new_client_research_uncovers_drivers_of_engagement_satisfaction_and_willingness_to_refer/prweb16293766.htm

Pentland, Alex. "The New Science of Building Great Teams." *Harvard Business Review* (April 2012).

Prince, Russ Alan and Brett Van Bortel. "Ways to Retain Top Clients Before They Leave." *Financial Advisor* (January 2018).

Summerhawk, Kendall. "Sacred Money Archetypes." https://sacredmoneyarchetypes.com

Verducci, Tom. "Unbreakable: The Red Sox's Season for the Ages." *Sports Illustrated* (October 2018).

Willis, Janine and Alexander Todorov. "First Impressions: Making Up Your Mind After a 100-Ms Exposure to a Face." Psychological Science 17, no. 7 (July 2006): 592-598.

"Workplace Conflict and How Businesses Can Harness It To Thrive." *CPP Global Human Capital Report* (July 2008).

Zander, Rosamund and Benjamin Zander. *The Art of Possibility.* New York, NY. Penguin Books, 2002.

Zenger, Jack and Joseph Folkman. "What Great Listeners Actually Do." *Harvard Business Review*, (July 2016).

ENDNOTES

1 Lieberman, Matthew D. *Why Our Brains Are Wired to Connect* (New York, NY: Crown Publishers, 2013)

2 Glaser, Judith. *Conversational Intelligence*. Brookline, MA: Bibliomotion, Inc., 2014.

3 Green, Mitchell, "Speech Acts", The Stanford Encyclopedia of Philosophy (Winter 2017 Edition), Edward N. Zalta (ed.), https://plato.stanford.edu/archives/win2017/entries/speech-acts/.

4 Goleman, Daniel. *Emotional Intelligence: Why It Can Matter More Than IQ* (New York, NY, Bantam Books, 1995)

5 Dimoka, Angelika. "What Does the Brain Tell Us About Trust and Distrust? Evidence from a Functional Neuroimaging Study." (*Management Information Systems Quarterly* 34 (2010).

6 Maxfield, David. "How a Culture of Silence Eats Away At Your Company." *Harvard Business Review* (December 2016).

7 Glaser, Judith. "Why You're Talking Past Each Other, and How to Stop." Harvard Business Review, (December 2012).

8 Flaum, J.P., "When it Comes to Business Leadership, Nice Guys Finish First." *Green Peak Partners* (2010). http://greenpeakpartners.com/wp-content/uploads/2018/09/

Green-Peak_Cornell-University-Study_What-predicts-success.pdf

9 Goleman, Daniel. *Working with Emotional Intelligence* (New York, NY: Bantam Books, 1998).

10 Lieberman, Matthew D. *Why Our Brains Are Wired to Connect* (New York, NY: Crown Publishers, 2013).

11 Nicklas Balboa and Richard D. Glaser, Ph.D., "The Neuroscience of Conversations." *Psychology Today*, (May 2019).

12 Eurich, Tasha. "What Self Awareness Really Is." *Harvard Business Review* (January 4, 2018).

13 Summerhawk, Kendall. "Sacred Money Archetypes." https://sacaredmoneyarchetypes.com

14 R. F. Baumeister and Mark R. Leary, "The Need to Belong: Desire for Interpersonal Attachments as a Fundamental Human Motivation." *Psychological Bulletin* 117, no. 3 (1995): 497-529.

15 Edmondson, Amy and Kathryn Roloff. "Leveraging Diversity Through Psychological Safety." *Rotman Magazine* (2009).

16 Edmondson, Amy. "Psychological Safety and Learning Behavior in Work Teams." *Administrative Quarterly* 44, no. 3 (1999):350-383.

17 Pentland, Alex. "The New Science of Building Great Teams." *Harvard Business Review* (April 2012).

18 Investment and Wealth Management, 2019 Research, "New Client Research Uncovers Drivers of Engagement, Satisfaction, and Willingness to Refer."

19 Hargie, Owen. Skilled Interpersonal Interaction: Research, Theory, and Practice, (London: Routledge, 2017).

20 Willis, Janine and Alexander Todorov, "First Impressions: Making Up Your Mind After a 100-Ms Exposure to a Face," Princeton University, (2005).

21 Littlechild, Julie. Investments and Wealth Institute Special Report, 2020 Investor Research, "The Current Crisis, The Impact on Client Loyalty, and the Implications for Your Business."

22 Jack Zenger and Joseph Folkman, "What Great Listeners Actually Do," *Harvard Business Review*, (July 2016).

23 Zander, Rosamund and Benjamin Zander. *The Art of Possibility* (New York, NY: Penguin Books, 2002).

24 Lencioni, Patrick. *The Five Dysfunctions of a Team*. (San Francisco, CA: Jossey-Bass, 2002).

25 Dalio, Ray. *Principles* (New York, NY: Simon and Schuster, 2017).

26 Brown, Brene. *Daring Greatly* (New York, NY: Penguin Random House, 2012).

27 Brown, Brene. *Rising Strong* (New York, NY: Penguin Random House, 2015).

28 Gino, Francesca. "The Business Case for Curiosity." (*Harvard Business Review* September-October, 2018).

29 Medina, John. *Brain Rules*, (Seattle, WA: Pear Press, 2014).

30 Verducci, Tom. "Unbreakable: The Red Sox's Season for the Ages." *Sports Illustrated*, (October 2018).

31 Edmondson, Amy. "Psychological Safety and Learning Behavior in Work Teams," Administrative Quarterly 44, no. 3 (1999):350-383.

32 "Workplace Conflict and How Businesses Can Harness It To Thrive." *CPP Global Human Capital Report*, (July 2008).

33 Prince, Russ Alan and Brett Van Bortel. "Ways to Retain Top Clients Before They Leave," *Financial Advisor*, (January 2018).

34 Naomi I. Eisenberger and Steve W. Cole, "Social neuroscience and health: neurophysiological mechanisms linking social ties with physical health." *Nature Neuroscience*, (May 2012).

35 Mann, Ann Marie and Nate Dvorak. "Employee Recognition: Low Cost, High Impact." *Gallup Workplace*, (June 2016).

36 Ghosh, Prarthana. "The Future of Work: 10 Key Trends for the Next 10 Years." *HR Technologist*, (July 2019).

37 Naomi I. Eisenberger and Steve W. Cole, "Social neuroscience and health: neurophysiological mechanisms linking social ties with physical health." *Nature Neuroscience*, (May 2012).

Made in the USA
Middletown, DE
17 June 2024